FAMILY POLICY PARADOXES

Gender equality and labour market regulation in Sweden, 1930-2010

Åsa Lundqvist

First published in Great Britain in 2011 by

The Policy Press
University of Bristol
Fourth Floor
Beacon House
Queen's Road
Bristol BS8 1QU
UK

t: +44 (0)117 331 4054
f: +44 (0)117 331 4093
tpp-info@bristol.ac.uk
www.policypress.co.uk

North American office:
The Policy Press
c/o International Specialized Books Services (ISBS)
920 NE 58th Avenue, Suite 300
Portland, OR 97213-3786, USA
t: +1 503 287 3093
f: +1 503 280 8832
info@isbs.com

British Library Cataloguing in Publication Data
A catalogue record for this book is available from the British Library.

Library of Congress Cataloging-in-Publication Data
A catalog record for this book has been requested.

ISBN 978 1 84742 455 6 hardcover

Cover design by The Policy Press
Front cover: image kindly supplied by Bharatha Kumar
Printed and bound in Great Britain by TJ International, Padstow
The Policy Press uses environmentally responsible print partners

FSC
www.fsc.org
MIX
Paper from
responsible sources
FSC® C013056

In memory of my mother and father,
Gunilla and Inge Lundqvist,
and to Markus, Sebastian and Sofie,
with love

Contents

Acknowledgements

Writing this book has been a great challenge for me. I would not have managed without my friends and colleagues, whose insights, concerns and intellectual stimulation have been of vital importance to the whole project. Thank you all.

I am particularly grateful to Professor Leonore Davidoff, who was the first to suggest that I could write a book in English about my research. You actually believed I could do it, and you gave me the necessary intellectual and personal support to do it. Thank you so much.

I am also sincerely indebted to Arnlaug Leira, Christine Roman and Birte Siim, who commented on early versions of different chapters. Their critical, experienced and at the same time encouraging reading of those texts gave me the nerve and inspiration to move on. Mats Benner has read and commented on many different versions of the whole manuscript many times. Always watchful in relation to my texts and full of enthusiasm for my projects and ideas, Mats is the one of the best readers in the world. Janet Fink and Diana Mulinari read the whole manuscript at the end of the writing process. I am deeply grateful for Janet's distinct, careful and highly constructive comments, which provided me with the essential tools for rewriting the manuscript. Diana's inspiring and thought-provoking remarks were invaluable for finishing the book. I have also benefited greatly from the intellectual stimulation and wonderful friendship from colleagues across different countries and academic departments. Early versions of the empirical findings were thoroughly discussed by the participants of the Anglo-Nordic Research Network on Kinship, Family and Policy, and I would like to thank them for sharing their wealth of knowledge on family and social policy with me. I am indebted to the participants in the comparative research project Gender Equality as a Perspective on Welfare: The Limits of Political Ambition, coordinated by Kari Melby, for providing such an inspiring and accommodating environment in which to consider and debate gender equality policies across Scandinavia. I am also grateful for the cooperation of my colleagues within the Nordic Centre of Excellence: The Nordic Welfare State – Historical Foundations and Future Challenges programme, coordinated by Pauli Kettunen. Funding from this programme allowed me to spend the autumn of 2008 in Norway (Trondheim) and the spring of 2009 in Denmark (Odense), where parts of this book were written. I am genuinely obliged to Kari Melby at the Department of Interdisciplinary Studies of Culture at Trondheim University in Norway and to Klaus Petersen at the Centre for Welfare State Research at Odense University in Denmark for their generous hospitality and for letting me be part of their stimulating and exciting academic milieus.

I also benefited from the discussions and academic work of Trine Annfelt, Anette Borchorst, Christina Carlsson Wetterberg, Sara Edenheim, Sara Eldén, Johanna Esseveld, Anna Jansdotter, Pauli Kettunen, Tina Mattsson, Anu Pylkännen, John Stewart, Anna-Birte Ravn and Bente Rosenbeck.

My deepest gratitude goes to Karen Bowler, commissioning editor, Leila Ebrahimi, editorial assistant, Laura Greaves, production editor, and to the copy editor at The Policy Press, for their enthusiasm and professional support during the entire project. Thank you also to the anonymous reviewer for helpful comments.

This book has been written with financial support from The Bank of Sweden Tercentenary Foundation (J2004-0231) and the Swedish Research Council.

Most of all, and with love and affection, thank you Mats and thank you Markus, Sebastian and Sofie, for sharing your lives with me.

Abbreviations

AK	Andra Kammaren (Second Chamber of Parliament)
AMS	Arbetsmarknadsverket (National Labour Market Board)
FK	Första kammaren (First Chamber of Parliament)
LO	Landsorganisationen (Swedish Trade Union Confederation)
SACO	Sveriges akademikers central organisation (Swedish Confederation of Professional Associations)
SAF	Svenska Arbetsgivareföreningen (Swedish Employers' Federation)
SAP	Socialdemokratiska Arbetarepartiet (Social Democratic Party)
Skr.	Skrivelse (memorandum)
SOU	Statens offentliga utredningar (government commission reports)
TCO	Tjänstemännens centralorganisation (Central Organisation of Salaried Employees)

ONE

Introduction: understanding the political regulation of the family

Feminists across nations demand gender equality. Resistance against long-lasting patterns of inequality in society, at work and within the family is growing. New patterns of gender relations prevail across Europe and serve as examples of the ongoing resistance against gender inequalities. Female employment continues to expand. As a result, the male-breadwinner model has lost its dominance throughout Europe, albeit with considerable variations between member states (Crompton, 1999, 2006; Daly, 2000; Lewis, 2001, 2003, 2009; Hantrais, 2004; Lewis and Giullari, 2005). Men no longer necessarily have sole responsibility for the household's income, and women are no longer the sole providers of (unpaid) household labour and childcare. The hegemony of the nuclear family has also been shaken, if not dethroned, by, for example, rising numbers of single mothers and of new family forms (Hobson, 1990; Silva and Smart, 1999; Björnberg and Kollind, 2003). On the basis of these tendencies, some observers speak about a shift from the male-breadwinner model to an 'adult worker model' (Lewis and Giullari, 2005).[1]

Balancing work and family life has in this context emerged as one of the most pressing political concerns in Europe today. How can European welfare states cope with the current and future needs of working parents for childcare, parental insurance or, for that matter, care of their own parents? EU member states all address these issues in a wide variety of ways.

Against this background, Nordic family policy has – and not for the first time in history – come into the international limelight. Of particular interest is the assumed connection between labour market participation, fertility rates (and family relations) and gender equality. Here, the Nordic countries stand out in an international comparison, with parallel high levels of female labour market participation and fertility. This pattern may be seen as an outcome of political initiatives to offer generous, gender-neutral parental insurance and publicly funded, high-quality childcare, as well as a general emphasis on gender equality throughout public policy (Ellingsæter and Leira, 2007).

A significant feature of the development of Nordic welfare policies is the importance attributed to female employment. The notion of the 'gender-equal family' and the discourse on gender neutrality emerged with the growing labour shortages and the development of the so-called sex-role debate in the 1960s (Dahlström et al, 1962; Hirdman, 1990, 1998; Acker et al, 1992; Baude, 1992; Florin and Karlsson, 2000; Leira, 2002; Roman, 2008). A practical outcome of the change in political discourse towards gender neutrality was a series of political initiatives to lower women's thresholds to the labour market, including massive investment in state childcare and the introduction of a gender-neutral parental insurance. Other elements included individual taxation and the legalisation of abortion, and, in Sweden, the emergence of gender equality policy as a political realm in itself (Åström, 1990; Hirdman, 1990; Elgàn, 1994; Florin, 1999; Ravn, 2008).

From the end of the 1960s, an increase in the number of opportunities for women to participate more fully in public life enabled increased equality for mothers with small children in both the workplace and at home; these were not only political goals in themselves but a manifestation of the strength of the women's movement in the Nordic countries (Melby et al, 2008). Transformed family relations and gender roles also became building blocks in a political programme for productivity and economic growth. Such a model has been described as a specifically Nordic – or, sometimes, social democratic – welfare regime in comparative studies of welfare policies (Hernes, 1988; Esping-Andersen, 1990, 2002; Sainsbury, 1996, 1999; Daly, 2000; Daly and Rake, 2001; Leira, 2002; Ellingsæter and Leira, 2007). In the realm of family and gender relations, such a regime is characterised by its stress on the integration of women in the labour market as a means to enhance gender equality and at the same time support and sustain economic growth (Ellingsæter, 1998; Morgan, 2005, 2006; Lundqvist, 2007, 2008). This has been a defining feature of Nordic welfare policies since the 1960s, although its more concrete forms have fluctuated, based on changing economic and political conditions, and it has taken a different shape within each Nordic country (see, for example, Leira, 1992, 2002; Bergqvist et al, 1999; Borchorst, 2005, 2008; Christiansen et al, 2006; Ellingsæter and Leira, 2007; Melby et al, 2008).

However, the notion of the gender-equal family has a longer history, going back to the 1930s and the interventions made by, among others, the influential social democratic intellectual Alva Myrdal (Myrdal, 1932, 1944). At an early stage, policy reforms aimed to halt decreasing birth rates and reduce social inequalities, introducing antenatal clinics and child welfare centres, means-tested maternity support, and the payment of the universal child allowance directly to the mother in 1948. Universal maternity support was introduced in the 1950s, at the same time as the debate on women's two roles, as mothers and workers, escalated (Klein and Myrdal, 1957). These family policy reforms were undertaken long before the radicalisation of the 1960s, which is important to bear in mind when considering the political processes shaping the contemporary family policy agenda. Thus the mounting ambitions of Swedish family policy from the 1960s onwards did not emerge out of a political vacuum; its origins go back (at least) to the 1930s.

This book explores the political regulation of the family in Sweden. More specifically, it is devoted to the historical development of family policy and the ensuing institutionalisation of gender equality in that context. The analysis begins in the 1930s when the family became an increasingly important reform object within the political sphere, and goes all the way to 2010 when family relations remains a key part of the interface between family policy, gender equality and labour market policy.

Historically, family policy in Sweden has been intertwined with gender equality ambitions. This combination has, however, not always been stable or easy to establish. Instead, tensions between family policy reforms and other fields such as social and labour market policy have recurred, shaping the norms, values and political outcomes of family policy regulation.

Paradoxes in the history of Swedish family policy

Family policy has not developed as a separate or isolated political domain. On the contrary, family policy cuts across several policy spheres. The early reforms described earlier were embedded in a broader political programme, sometimes called the Swedish model. The concept refers to the economic and social ambition to modernise Swedish society in the post-war period through a renewal of labour market relations, new models for the management of economic swings, reduced social inequalities and reforms of family and gender relations. Moreover, social equality was to be combined with full employment, rapid growth increases and macroeconomic stringency with low inflation. The foundation was a combination of a Keynesian stabilisation policy to manage economic fluctuations without cost-push inflation with a selective labour market policy for labour mobility, reducing bottlenecks in the labour market (Rothstein, 1996; Benner, 1997). As time went on, the ambitions were widened and an increasing number of policy areas were drawn into the modernisation programme: schooling and higher education, environmental protection, industrial and regional development, and foreign aid, to mention just a few (Therborn, 1989; Rothstein, 1992, 1996; Åmark, 2005). In this model, family and gender equality policies served as a means to adjust conditions between women and men in the labour market as well as within the family. Equal opportunities between women and men thus became part of the Swedish model at an early stage.

Family policy reforms played an increasingly central role in the modernisation of Sweden in the 20th century. The family moved from a peripheral political role to the centre of political life: not only its social and economic conditions but its very forms and functions became objects of political intervention. What emerged out of this was a complex, and sometimes contradictory and paradoxical, interplay between gender equality, social policy reforms and labour market regulation.

Family policy as it emerged in the 1930s was first of all a response to decreasing fertility rates and alarming poverty levels among families with children. By introducing policy reforms aimed at improving living conditions among poor women and men, the family became an object of political intervention. Women were the primary object of reform policies; in the attempts to establish better conditions for poor families, women's role as mothers and carers in the home as well as workers was emphasised. This highlights the first, and perhaps the most long-lasting paradox in modern family policy: that of work and family life. The relationship between work and family also represents the paradox of equality and difference; in theory, all citizens were to be treated equally, but in political practice, selected groups such as (poor) women were targeted in political reforms. Even 'racial hygiene' ideals were introduced and conceptualised as an improvement of the population quality.

In post-war Sweden, the paradox of work and family deepened. Ambivalent family ideals developed alongside the introduction of family policy reforms. Some argued that women's conditions in the labour market had to be improved through the expansion of state childcare, while others pledged for the importance of a caring, stay-at-home mother in order to secure the future of society. Indeed, the paradox of women's two roles became a troublesome issue for politicians in the immediate post-war period, although it was partly politically solved during the 1960s by the introduction of the gender-equal family.

All that is solid melts into air. The so-called sex-role debate in the 1960s contributed to a reorientation and renegotiation of what a family really was, and what it meant to be a woman and a man: sex roles were considered not to be a natural given order, but socially constructed. Following this analysis, the political focus gradually changed from the mother to both men and women as providers of caring work. Gender neutrality, introduced mainly through initiatives such as individual taxation, parental leave insurance and the new marriage law, and the gender-equal family became lead themes in family policy, making men targets for family policy reforms for the first time in history. At the same time, a new policy area emerged, namely the field of gender equality policy.

Thus, despite the combined effects of a financial and ideological crisis, the decade was a harvest period for family policy. The ideals of the dual-earner family and shared caring responsibilities were, after almost three decades, shaping social policy and labour market policy. This turned out to be an irreversible change as these ideals continue to inform family policy. The assumed mutually reinforcing relationship between gender-equal relations, economic growth and full employment continues to be a political cornerstone, irrespective of ideological shifts and political swings.

However, the gender-equal family and gender-neutral policy reforms were soon to be criticised, not least because of an in-built paradox: during the 1980s, feminist research showed that women were still the primary carers in the homes, despite all reforms and legislation – there was gender equality and gender neutrality on a legislative level but gender discrimination and segregation remained in working life and unequal patterns prevailed in family relations. The feminist critique of family- and gender-equal policies has resulted in recurrent attempts to regulate unequal relations between women and men, in family life and at work. In these attempts, new paradoxes have emerged. One prime example is the cash-for-care system, aiming to support a stay-at-home parent and to support private day-care provision, in a family policy system where all other reforms are constructed to facilitate gainful employment for both women and men.

In general, however, the debates and political praxis behind gender equality policy and family policy reforms do not differ much between governments. On the contrary, gender equality ideals are shared among all established political parties. This idea is, however, based on the paradoxical notion of enforcing gender equality while maintaining the independence and autonomy of women and men.

Why Sweden?

In the Swedish context, ideologies of gender equality and family policies are intertwined. Since the 1960s, attempts to regulate family life have been based on the assumption that family members are better off in gender-equal relations. In addition, an emphasis on full employment that promotes the concept of working mothers has marked the way in modern Swedish history. This, together with highlighting the role of the state in, for example, caring for children in publicly funded day-care centres, illuminates a tradition where the public–private divide has been in some ways transcended (compare Leira, 2002). In this context, the role of the father has also become a priority in the attempt to achieve gender-equal relations. This development distinguishes Sweden (and the Nordic countries) from most other western welfare states.

Indeed, there has been a long tradition of rethinking the family and family relations in Nordic politics, particularly in Sweden, not least because some of the earliest and perhaps most influential thinkers in the field, such as Alva Myrdal and sociologist Rita Liljeström, were Swedish.

Thus, several factors point to the centrality of the Swedish experience. Moreover, family and gender relations are important political issues for states all over the world. Many of the initiatives adopted by other countries use Sweden as their inspiration, although the Swedish experience sometimes serves as a cautionary tale of political failure (Esping-Andersen, 1990, 2002). The Swedish case is also cited in many cross-cultural studies of family regulation and gender equality, mainly because of its exceptional character and its alleged – mainly by its government – stability and productivity. Moreover, Sweden, together with its Nordic neighbours, is often at the top in benchmarking exercises, such as the World Economic Forum's Gender Gap Index 2007 and the Organisation for Economic Co-operation and Development (OECD) 2007 list of the most gender-equal countries.

However, most studies related to the political regulation of the family and gender-equal policies are concerned with contemporary developments and offer few historical insights or in-depth analysis of the Swedish experience. As a result, the Swedish legacy of paradoxes, ambiguities and contradictions within policy formation remains a little understood subtext. This study intends to fill this gap by examining the development of a complex political model and the attempt to regulate the family and establish gender equality.

Mapping the field: starting points and theoretical inspiration

This study is concerned with the political regulation of the family. There is a vast amount of research on how welfare states of various designs regulate families and their behaviour. Later, I discuss the debates surrounding the state–family interface and the key concepts in the literature, indicating how these debates and concepts have informed and shaped my own analytical scheme and interpretations in the empirical chapters.

Gender, work and welfare regimes

> Gender relations, embodied in the sexual division of labor, compulsory heterosexuality, discourses and ideologies of citizenship, motherhood, masculinity and femininity, and the like, profoundly shape the character of welfare states. Likewise, the institutions of social provision – the set of social assistance and social insurance programs, universal citizenship, entitlements, and public services to which we refer as 'the welfare state' – affect gender relations in a variety of ways. (Orloff, 1996, p 51)

Gender relations and the family have always been central in studies of social policy and the welfare state. In early studies with a conservative bent, the cold and instrumental ways of the welfare state have been pitted against the nurturing power of the family. From a radically different perspective, critical feminists in the 1970s and the 1980s claimed that this understanding of the family was skewed – far from being 'the haven in a heartless world' (Lasch, 1977), it reproduced uneven gender power relations. Not only did it reproduce inequality, but it also served as a foundation for the production of a sexist ideology (Barrett and McIntosh, 1982). The (welfare) state acted, by definition, as a guarantor of reproduced inequalities and thereby of unequal relations between women and men. Several mechanisms served to reproduce gender inequalities, among them segregation in the labour market, tax legislation and the male-centred marriage contract (Gordon, 1988). Another element, highlighted by Scandinavian feminists, was the degradation of care work in comparison with male-dominated sectors in the labour market (Wærness, 1984).[2] Thus, early feminist analysis of gender relations, work and the (welfare) state focused on the repressive functions of the state.

In 1990, Gøsta Esping-Andersen presented his widely used and contested typology. He distinguished between three welfare regimes: liberal, conservative and social democratic. Regimes types were constructed on the basis of an intricate relationship between institutions and outcomes: the interaction between states, markets and families, the provision of social services and social insurances, and the impact of policies on inequalities and employment (Esping-Andersen, 1990).

The social democratic regime, to which the Scandinavian countries squarely belong, is characterised by the combination of universal access to tax-financed social services with income-based social insurances. It is also the regime with the strongest redistributive effects, which has been interpreted as a sign of the political strength of egalitarian values (Sainsbury, 1996, 1999; Kautto et al, 1999). Thus, the social democratic regime 'crowds out the market, and consequently constructs an essential universal solidarity in favour of the welfare state. All benefit, all are dependent; and will presumably feel obliged to pay' (Esping-Andersen, 1990, p 28).

The concepts of commodification and decommodification – first introduced by Karl Polanyi (1944) – are central to Esping-Andersen's analysis of regime types. Commodification refers to the wage–labour nexus – where social rights are related to labour market participation. Decommodification, as a mirror concept, refers to access to services irrespective of labour market participation, 'when a person can maintain a livelihood without reliance on the market' (Esping-Andersen, 1990, pp 21-2). As can be seen, welfare and labour market participation are knitted together in Esping-Andersen's typology. This assumption has been the subject of much criticism over the years. A core criticism was afforded by Jane Lewis, who stressed the gender blindness of the typology, neglecting the relationship between paid and unpaid labour, as well as the multifaceted provision of social services (Lewis, 1992, 1997). Lewis was also critical of the use of decommodification as an indicator of the strength of the welfare state:

> Commodification has proved difficult for many women seeking a degree of autonomy via wage-earning, while de-commodification via social-security systems is likely to result in women carrying out unpaid work. In other words, 'welfare dependency' on the part of adult women is likely to result in the greater independence of another person, young or old. (Lewis, 2000, p 38)

Jane Lewis developed an alternative typology taking account of these shortcomings. In this 'breadwinner typology', there are 'strong male-breadwinner states' (exemplified by the UK), 'modified male-breadwinner states' (France) and 'weak male-breadwinner states' (Sweden). All welfare states are variants of a male-breadwinner model, but to highly variable degrees. The predominant indicators of the strength of breadwinner models were the integration of women in the labour market, the design of social insurances and taxation, and the provision of state childcare (Lewis, 1992, 1997).[3] Lewis argued that the theorising of welfare state typologies should benefit from analysing these variations, or we might overlook 'one of the central issues in the structuring of welfare regimes: the problem of valuing the unpaid work that is done primarily by women in providing welfare, mainly within the family, and in securing those providers' social entitlements' (Lewis, 1992, p 160).

It should be noted that the Nordic social democratic welfare (breadwinner) regime is not a uniform entity. The Norwegian sociologist Anne-Lise Ellingsæter has shown how the Scandinavian countries have differed in their paths away from the male-breadwinner model (Ellingsæter, 1998). While they are all 'modified' dual-breadwinner societies, where women have taken a prominent position in public policy and in the labour market, the differences are reflected in wide variations in the design of parental insurance, in the organisation of childcare and in policies for female employment (Ellingsæter, 1998). With regard to the latter, Swedish and Norwegian policies have targeted the provision of part-time work for women, while Danish policies have targeted full-time employment. On the other hand, the political attitudes to working mothers are more ambivalent in Norway than in Sweden and Denmark (Leira, 1992).

The analysis of regime typologies has also led to a rethinking of how welfare states cluster, by asking whether it is possible to identify 'caring regimes' as a point of departure. Inspired by Esping-Andersen's typology, two Finnish researchers, Anneli Anttonen and Jorma Sipilä (1996), studied a number of western European countries in order to investigate how different welfare states handle public and private responsibilities in relation to caring for children and the older population. Their analysis show that if care is included as a theoretical concept, the outcome of how welfare states cluster will be different from Esping-Andersen's. For example, Norway is not a part of the Scandinavian model, since state provision for children is in short supply. Instead, Norway is classed with the UK and the Netherlands. Sweden, on the other hand, has abundant services available for both young and old (as have Denmark and Finland) (Anttonen and Sipilä, 1996).

The analysis made by Anttonen and Sipilä relies heavily on the development of the concept of care, a debate that has changed our thinking about the relationship between paid and unpaid work and between public and private responsibilities and about how gender relations are shaped within these dichotomies. This debate will be the topic of the next section.

Gender and care

The concept of care has been widely debated in the Scandinavian context. It has also been used in welfare studies, although with some variations and with different meanings attached to it. It first emerged in feminist studies, and has been extensively used and developed in welfare studies of the Scandinavian countries (and the UK). In welfare studies, it initially denoted female experiences of caring, but has later been widened to encompass service provision. One of the pioneers in research on caring, the Norwegian sociologist Kari Wærness (1984), showed that women had been constructed as having the main responsibility for unpaid care work. Another Norwegian sociologist, Arnlaug Leira, later conducted a study of working mothers in Scandinavia, arguing that their caring work was conducted within relations of 'personal ties of obligation, commitment, trust and loyalty. The process of care was emphasized and explored in terms of loving, thinking and doing' (Leira, 1992, p 27). In an early account of the position of the welfare state within different 'caring regimes', Leira related caring work to publicly organised care, for instance in childcare and care for the elderly (see also Borchorst and Siim, 1987, for an analysis of care outside the home as a form of 'public patriarchy').

In a later study, Leira put together different factors in women's and men's lives and argued that the concept of employed parents as wage workers, carers of children and citizens of welfare states constitutes the main criterion by which mothers and fathers can claim their rights in a welfare state: 'As a citizen, the employed parent is entitled to claim the social right universally available, and as a worker has access to employment-related services and benefits. What care-related social rights might actually be is often less well defined' (Leira, 2002, p 7). However, Leira argues, in recent times care-related rights have often included benefits in cash and access to services, as well as the right to be (and the right not to be full time) a carer of children.

Mary Daly and Jane Lewis (2000) put the concept of care at the centre of studies of welfare states, and described 'the way in which social care lies at the intersection of public and private (in the sense of both state/family and state/market provision); formal and informal; paid and unpaid; and provision in the form of cash and services' (Daly and Lewis, 2000, p 282). They also pointed out the multifaceted forms of care: being both paid and unpaid, shaped by emotional experiences and normative concerns, and embedded in social and economic practice (Daly and Lewis, 2000, p 285).

However, the Scandinavian countries' experience as 'women-friendly states' has had a strong influence on theoretical and empirical studies of caring models, given their commitment to female employment and the provision of state care. The organisation of care in these respects has been a central issue in Swedish family policy, and one of the main aims of this study will therefore be to elucidate how care work has been understood and 'managed' over the decades in question.

A woman-friendly welfare state?

> The Scandinavian welfare states have been labelled as woman-friendly, and this terms implies that they have been responsive towards women's claims, given them a voice and adopted a range of policies that increased women's options. (Borchorst, 2009, p 2)

As far back as the 1930s, Alva Myrdal claimed that men and women should share responsibility for their children; in the modern world, families could not afford to live unequal lives – democracy demanded equality (Myrdal, 1932). Some years later, Myrdal, together with her British colleague Viola Klein, wrote in a book entitled *Women's Two Roles* (Klein and Myrdal, 1957) that mothers of small children should be given time for gainful employment and that society should make this possible for them. But men's role as breadwinners was still undisputed. However, in the 1970s, the Swedish family sociologist, Rita Liljeström, presented her model of shared societal roles where mothers and fathers were equally responsible for both breadwinning and parenting. Following the so-called sex-role debate (that she had been a part of) from the 1960s, Liljeström claimed that the time was ripe for a dual-earner, care-sharing family. Such a family was dependent on an active welfare state to facilitate gainful employment for both mothers and fathers (Liljeström, 1978). During the 1980s, it actually seemed as if the Scandinavian family was 'going public'. A series of political initiatives were taken to support dual-breadwinner families, the most noteworthy being a massive expansion of state childcare (Leira, 1992, 2002). While conservative critics interpreted this as a suppression of traditional family values, others perceived its women-friendly potential:

> A woman-friendly state would enable women to have a natural relationship to their children, their work and public life….A woman-friendly state would not force harder choices on women than on men, or permit unjust treatment on the basis of sex. In a woman-friendly state women will continue to have children, yet there will also be other roads to self-realization open to them. (Hernes, 1987, p 15)

The Norwegian political scientist Helga Hernes argued that female public citizenship, and a women-friendly state, could only be realised if social reproduction were made public. The expansion of state childcare, and the increase in opportunities for women to participate more fully in public life, was the centrepiece of women-friendly policies and set the Scandinavian countries apart in international comparisons (compare Borchorst and Siim, 2009).

It has been argued, however, that the gains are conditional, even in Scandinavia (compare Leira, 2002). One of the driving forces behind the partial retrenchment has been the rise of new public management ideologies, emphasising 'the freedom to choose' in social care. The introduction of a cash-for-care scheme (*vårdnadsbidrag*) in Norway (1998) and Sweden (first in 1994 for only six months and then in 2008) was premised on the notion of free choice, affording families a state-subsidised alternative to state childcare. In effect, this paved the way for a more complex analysis of the welfare state:

> The Scandinavian welfare states have come far in terms of providing public child-care and granting generous parental leave schemes. However, the process toward 'reproduction going public' has not taken a linear form in the manner Hernes anticipated and there is a growing awareness that the boundary between public and private is fluid and socially constructed. The public/private divide is subject to conflicts, negotiation, and various framings. (Borchorst and Siim, 2009, p 215)

Hernes's study was not the only analysis of the Scandinavian model offered in the 1980s. A rather radical reinterpretation of the history of Swedish welfare policies in particular was offered by the Swedish historian Yvonne Hirdman (1988, 1989, 1990). In her analysis of the emergence of the welfare state, she showed that women's experiences as mothers and carers were seen as problematic by leading social democrats. A strong driving force behind all welfare policies therefore became to create – by rational planning – a place for women as carers in a welfare state organised around paid labour and economic growth. In this position, women became citizens on men's terms, Hirdman argued (1989). Hirdman's analysis can be seen as an intervention against social democratic hegemony in defining and solving policy dilemmas, paving the way for a more complex discourse and policy practice in Swedish family and gender equality policies.

The debate about whether the welfare state should be explained in terms of women-friendliness or as a repressive force coincided with the entrance of neoliberalism and the re-emergence of the family sociology in the international debate.

By having relied heavily on structural-functionalist theories such as those of Talcott Parsons, family sociology seemed to have been phased out as a research field in the 1970s and the 1980s (replaced by feminist research on power relations between women and men). This changed in the 1990s. Relating economic globalisation and the rise of a 'new economy' to de-traditionalisation and new family relations, sociologists Anthony Giddens, Ulrich Beck and Elisabeth Beck-Gernsheim moved into the field, making it the new centrepiece in sociological theorising (Giddens, 1991, 1992; Beck, 1992, 2002; Beck-Gernsheim, 2002). In late-modern societies, it was argued, hitherto stable social categories like class, gender and religious belonging were undermined by the increasing flexibility and volatility of economic, cultural and political relations. The impact was particularly felt in the individual biography, where self-realisation had become the overarching target. This had a major impact on family life. In what was proclaimed to be a 'self-reflexive' world, a negotiated and democratic family model was emerging in which the gender division of labour was blurred and families (and other social entities) consisted of self-reflexive individuals (Beck and Beck-Gernsheim, 1995).

These interventions certainly revitalised family sociology, but they were later put under empirical scrutiny. Empirical studies showed few signs of the emergence of a negotiated family structure or of the wide-ranging rise of the individual self-reflexive autobiography (Silva and Smart, 1999; Ahlberg et al, 2008). Family relations are still characterised by inequality, and social categories such as class, ethnicity and, for that matter, gender, still shape family practices.

> There may be de-traditionalization (for example more people may cohabit outside marriage, more children live in extended families) but this does not necessarily mean that individualization follows.... [S]ociologists have inaccurately conflated choice with agency, and underestimated structural conditions and their effects on actions. (Ahlberg et al, 2008, p 95)

The individualisation thesis, which emerged in parallel with the rise of neoliberalism, clearly related to family policy development in Sweden; individualisation was the dominant social condition in post-industrial Sweden, and was the motivation for initiatives such as gender-neutral parental insurance. At the same time, gender inequalities were explained as structural obstacles formed by the welfare state itself. This was translated into an ideology of women being subordinated to men as a group. This ideology became the lead theme of gender equality policies, and the resulting incoherence – indeed paradoxical relationship – between individualism and structuralism formed family policy throughout the 1990s. This development will be examined further in Chapter Five.

Gender equality and the 'diversity turn'

Gender equality policies have, as we have seen, a long tradition in the Nordic countries, from early 20th-century struggles for female suffrage to latter-day gender equality discourses and policies where individual rights have been disconnected from the family to a higher degree than in other states.[4] Gender equality is today an overarching political goal in Sweden. The centre-right government defined gender equality policies in the following manner in 2009:

> The government's gender-equality policy aims partly to counteract and change systems which conserve the gender distribution of power and resources at a societal level, partly to create equally good conditions for women and men to have the power and resources to shape their living conditions. When women and men share the power and responsibility in all parts of society we will have a more just and democratic society. By enhancing the competence and creativity of all people, gender equality also contributes to economic growth. (www. regeringen.se/sb/d/2593)

Gender equality policy therefore emerges as a policy umbrella and a key to both democratic development and economic growth (this development will be examined further in Chapter Five). This is also well in line with the central role of gender equality policy in Sweden. As discussed throughout this book, it has historically been tied to different policy areas, primarily labour market policy, family policy and social policy.

Gender equality policy has moved forward to the extent that gender relations, rather than the relationship between the classes, is now a dominant feature. In more recent years, it has expanded even further to encompass unequal relations based on sexuality, disability or ethnicity. As an indication of this widening definition, the gender discrimination ombudsman became the discrimination ombudsman in 2009, when the sexual discrimination, disability discrimination, ethnic discrimination and gender equality ombudsmen roles were merged.

There are in this respect, again, distinct differences between the Scandinavian countries. State feminism has featured more prominently in Sweden, where gender equality policy has been based on the assumption that it is targeting a structurally embedded phenomenon (Roman, 2008). This sets Sweden apart from both Denmark and Norway, where individual choice and inducible utility play a larger role both in the explanation of inequality and in the design of its remedies (Skeije and Teigen, 2003; Borchorst, 2004).

Of course, gender equality is not only a feature of Swedish, or Nordic, policy. It has also become a global political concept, with positive connotations, embraced by governments worldwide (Squires, 2007). Despite its rise in global prominence, however, its meaning in different policy contexts is variable. For the women's movement, gender equality was indeed a central political aim in its early phase, based on egalitarian conceptions of liberation from (state-supported) gender oppression. Gradually, its political goals came to embrace a broader set of political goals – domestic work, sexuality and reproduction (Fraser, 2007; Squires, 2007).

In the 1980s, as gender equality policy in this form was achieving serious political recognition, it was suddenly discredited. Not only did the rise of neoliberalism propel a growing suspicion of redistribution, but a politics of identity also came into being, appearing to 'frequently ... valorize cultural difference rather that promote economic equality' (Squires, 2007, p 7). At the same time, vociferous demands were being made to address women's political (under-)representation – partially as a response to the failure to alter power relations in the economic sphere. This ideological turn made class relations a less salient issue than gender relations to many western governments. Sweden is a case in point, as attention to political representation has grown dramatically here, leading to more balanced gender representation in parliament and government. However, the debate surrounding representation, as well as for equal representation in the parliament from the women's movement, has been developed in parallel with a somewhat different debate: the impact of immigration and the rise of a more diverse society:

> The Scandinavian population has become more diverse in terms of religion, culture and language. This development has raised critical questions about the ability of the Nordic welfare model to include immigrants in the labour market and about the normative foundations of the dominant Nordic model of gender equality and woman-friendliness. (Borchorst and Siim, 2009, p 221)

This corresponds to a more general development from equality to diversity, where the relationship and intersections between different layers and spheres (sexual, racial, religious, age-related and so on) form the basis of political action (Squires, 2007, p 16). This has proven to be a difficult transition for the Scandinavian countries (Siim, 2008), not least for Sweden.

For some time, Scandinavian equality policy has been the example that others have followed, and this is still perhaps the case. In a similar vein, Scandinavian integration policy has emerged as a policy showcase, primarily because of the (alleged) successful integration of immigrants in these states (Schierup et al, 2006). Swedish immigration policy is also rather generous by European standards, reflected in its ethnically relatively diverse population structure.

With intensifying economic growth and ensuing labour shortages in the 1950s and particularly the 1960s, labour market immigration took off in Sweden. The dominant migrant groups were Finnish, Italian, Greek, Turkish and Yugoslavian. Sweden diverged from the guest-worker approach of many other European countries and aimed at an inclusive stance, in which migrants were covered by the social insurance system, and were given the right to vote in local elections (Schierup et al, 2006). Nonetheless, the position of migrants in the labour market was weaker and more contingent than that of native Swedes, resulting in what has been described as 'subordinated inclusion' (Mulinari, 2008).

Labour market immigration ended in 1972. At the same time, the number of political refugees and asylum seekers increased dramatically, first from Chile, Iran, and the Horn of Africa and then, in the 1990s, the Balkans. Despite rising unemployment and right-wing attacks on immigration, Sweden established an 'anti-racist integration policy' in the late 1990s with broad-based political support, making Sweden 'unique in Europe, with its political compact committed to combating racialized exclusion' (Schierup et al, 2006, p 196). At the same time, ethnic segregation in the labour market had become even more institutionalised, leading to a paradoxical juxtaposition of a political commitment to diversity and increasing ethnic segmentation (Ålund and Schierup, 1991; Schierup et al, 2006).

The question of ethnicity and immigration has also been discussed in relation to gender equality. A repeated critique from post-colonial research has highlighted the limits of welfare state policies when it comes to migrants (Williams, 1997; Lewis, 1998). Welfare policies are founded on the notion and discourse that migrants are indifferent to widely cherished ideas of equality in general and gender equality in particular (Langvasbråten, 2008; Mulinari, 2008; Siim, 2008; Siim and Skeije, 2008).

It has been shown that gender equality policy in Sweden has incorporated ethnic diversity but that it is still strongly influenced by gender system thinking (where gender equality is based on the relationship between Swedish women and men). This has left other social categories, such as ethnicity and religion, in the political shadow (Langvasbråten, 2008). It is therefore important to highlight the close relationship between gender equality and the notion of the Swedish welfare state. In official documents and political debates, gender equality is not a matter of opinion – it has to do with knowledge and morality: 'Hence Swedes, in general are convinced that immigrants especially from outside of Europe need to be educated into Swedish ideals of gender equality' (Annika Rabo, cited in Mulinari, 2008, p 169). As a result, many immigrant women have ambivalent experiences of their meeting with welfare institutions. Mulinari again:

> While they [the immigrant women in her study] had to confront on a daily basis the discriminatory practices at the core of the Swedish ethnic and gender regimes, they also enjoyed many of the inclusive 'women-friendly' policies. In my view, these policies have been central in transforming gender relations in ways that, to a certain extent, empower women in the Latin American diaspora in Sweden. (Mulinari, 2008, p 180)

The other Scandinavian countries are even less influenced by ethnic diversity in their gender equality policies. Denmark has gone down a confrontational route where the values and norms of migrant women and men are pitted against those of 'gender-equal Danes'. This is particularly apparent in attitudes towards so-called honour-related violence. A similar pattern is discernible in Norway (Melby et al, 2008; Borchorst and Siim, 2009; Fink and Lundqvist, 2009, 2010).

This book analyses the relationship between family policy and diversity through the lenses of the political articulation and interpretation of gender equality as a specific Swedish experience, resulting in the emergence of cultural essentialism and structural discrimination.

Sources and methodological reflections

The study focuses on the political regulation of the family in Sweden between 1930 and 2010. It primarily aims to disentangle the complex and sometimes paradoxical relationship between ideologies and steering models in the development of family policy. A core feature of this development is the close relationship between policy making and social science analysis of gender and family relations.

This link with social science research is a unique feature of family policy in Sweden. Reforms have normally been inspired, or legitimated, by research in the social sciences (Hermansson, 1993). The setting for the interplay between politics and research are so-called government commissions. Not only do the commisssions' reports include findings from scientific experts, but also their proposals often echo these findings. Family and gender equality policies seek – and gain – the support of family studies. In this way, science and politics forge a strong relationship, which fosters post-war family policy. Thus, the relationship between science and politics is at the very centre of this analysis of family policy development.

In order to study the development of Swedish family policy, the specific features of the Swedish political system must therefore be taken into account. These include the important role of government commissions in policy formation. In Sweden, central ministries are relatively small, because policy implementation is the responsibility of independent government boards and agencies. The practice of preparing government proposals through ad hoc commissions has also contributed to the limited size of government administration. Furthermore, the central role played by ad hoc commissions and independent public agencies in the policy process means that experts and state officials have been very important policy shapers, especially in emerging fields like family policy (Lundqvist, 2007, 2008).

Hence, much of the study is based on material from these commissions, as they represent a unique window on the policy formation phase in Swedish politics. Parliamentary records and government Bills supplement this particular material.

Government commissions

Government commissions play a unique role in Swedish politics. Nowhere else, with the partial exception of Finland, are the reports of government commissions as important for the policy process as in Sweden (Johansson, 1991). Historically, the commissions have been relatively large and composed of a wide range of stakeholder representatives, including members of parliament, ministry officers, interest groups, civil servants and academic scholars. Through their participation in the commissions, all of these parties have been engaged from an early stage in the reform process.

The reports vary in content. Some are more like surveys of research relevant to a specific policy field with more general connections to policy making and reforms. Others serve as legitimisations of ensuing political reforms. Most reports, however, are blends of political negotiation and lengthy academic research reporting. In these cases, the commissions and their reports operate in the interstices between politics and expertise, negotiating political compromises and connecting academics with policymakers.

The period between 1930 and 1970, marked by the political dominance of social democracy, has been described as a relatively peaceful time when pragmatic negotiations shaped Swedish society (Korpi, 1983; Therborn, 1989; Åmark, 1998, 2005). A cornerstone in this societal model was the government commissions; their purpose was to create consensus among a broad array of stakeholders, and, furthermore, to base these compromises on knowledge provided by academic experts. Not only did politics become influenced by science, but science also became an integral part of policy making, drawing generations of social scientists into the policy-making machinery: 'The proposals of a government commission have sometimes been perceived as facts based on science.... From such a perspective the commissions appear as instruments for a scientific politics' (Johansson, 1991, p 13).

This study assumes that family policy has been shaped by the interplay between political regulation and academic expertise. In the heyday of the commissions (up to the mid-1970s), they served three functions:

- to produce knowledge that can enlighten political choices;
- to support the preparation and planning of political reforms;
- to create consensus in the policy-making process.

Eventually, these three aspects came into conflict. The biggest and final blow was the oil crises of the 1970s and the ensuing tightening of public expenditure. Political relations were also becoming more conflictual at the time and marked by fiercer ideological confrontations between the political parties, making consensus more unattainable. The social and economic turbulence also fostered a new politics of speed, where the commissions no longer had the time, nor the mandate, to commission large research projects. Some commissions had worked over several years, sometimes even decades, increasingly an anomaly in a political system searching for quick responses to changing circumstances (SOU 1985:40). Instead of basing their work on empirical studies and then presenting viable solutions, the commissions were often asked to provide a menu of policy alternatives. This diminished the experts' role as bridges between science and policy. Academic researchers had also cultivated a certain distance from the commissions, as the era of social engineering was coming to an end; they increasingly sought to develop an arm's-length relationship with politics (Lundqvist, 2007). Another element that, somewhat ironically, exacerbated the declining importance of the commissions was the expansion of the public sector, as growing state agencies developed in-house expertise and commissioned their own research projects (Stevrin, 1978). It seemed, then, as if the commissions had played out their role as consensus-making institutions in Swedish politics.

To sum up, in the period between 1930 and 1970, the commissions aligned politics with research; they commissioned research and prepared for coming political reforms, in this sense laying the foundation for a science-based policy consensus marked by rational policy making and balanced negotiations between different interest groups. This gave the commissions a unique position in the political landscape at the time. At the end of the 1970s, the role of the commissions changed, and researchers engaged in the commission system emphasised their independence. This does not mean that the government commission reports were less influential, but rather that researchers engaged in writing these reports considered themselves more independent, which in turn resulted in a reduction in science-based consensus in policy making.

Parliamentary records

The parliamentary records – the complete record of government Bills, motions and parliamentary debates – complement the analysis, as they document the political reception of the commission reports. This study focuses on a selected number of Bills, motions and debates. This enables a more thorough analysis of the policy impact of the commissions, as well as other influences in family policy making.

Delimitations

This study focuses on the regulation of Swedish family policy and the institutionalisation of gender equality. In doing so, it makes some demarcations. Family policy is not a clear-cut policy area, as the regulation of the family touches on virtually all policy fields. A pragmatic delimitation has therefore been made that incorporates some (but not all) debates on taxation policy, housing, childcare and so on; these are taken into account whenever debates in these areas contribute to the regulation of family relations (and vice versa). The selection is not entirely subjective, but based on recurrent themes (first, the design of parental support to mothers and later also fathers, and, second, the interface between paid labour and household and care work). By following these themes over time, the study traces continuities and changes in discourse and policy practice. As a contrast, issues that are specific for each of the periods under study have been included, to illustrate more time-bound arguments and debates.

The development of labour market regulation is presented in each chapter. These overviews serve as a way of describing the context in which family policy and gender equality reforms emerged, mainly because here the study departs from the view that these two policy fields are intertwined. However, labour market policy reforms are not analysed in an in-depth way: labour market laws and regulations are not described in detail. The reason lies in the fact that such an analysis could easily detract from the family policy development.

Quotations from government commissions, the parliamentary records and secondary sources in the following chapters illustrate or underline these analyses. Much of this material is originally written in Swedish, and throughout the book the translations are the author's own unless otherwise specified. The translation process has not been easy, especially considering the older texts, those from the 1930s for example. Commission reports and parliamentary records are written in old-fashioned Swedish and thereby conditioned by the period. When these sentences are translated into English, they lose some of their time-specific context. It is hoped, however, that the use of quotes will give the reader a feeling of the content of what was said and debated, rather that a stylistic and time-bound linguistic exposé of how policy making and debates were expressed.

As already mentioned, this book is about policy processes and the political regulation of the family. This means that family practices – how family policy reforms affect women and men in their everyday lives – are not analysed. The book's main concern is how political documents and debates have turned into policy reforms, shaping gender and family relations over time.

Structure of the book

The rest of the book is divided into five chapters and a conclusion. Chapter Two deals with the period between 1930 and 1940, a time when the family became an increasingly important reform object in Sweden. The period marks the beginning of the development of modern family policy, framed at the time as population policy. The dominant discourse – in politics as well as within the social sciences – stressed the functions of the nuclear family as a source of stability in the volatility that followed industrialisation. The model of the 'new family' was at the same time clearly influenced by ideas of equality. These ideas and discourses came to be outlined somewhat differently in policy praxis.

Several reforms were enacted in order to reduce widespread poverty and in an attempt to halt decreasing fertility levels, although it was only women who were targeted in family and social policy reforms. As a result of these reforms, the paradox of the work–family balance was born: policymakers stressed the importance of enabling mothers to take care of their children while implementing reforms to enhance women's position in the labour market.

At the same time, discussions on eugenics emerged, which were followed by legislation on sterilisation. Thus, the 1930s mirror the complex and paradoxical relationship between the concepts of equality and difference. Equality was emphasised in a more ideological way. In theory it was assumed that in a sophisticated, modern society all citizens should be equal, but in practical politics and discussions, differences were emphasised, for example in policies to improve social conditions for selected groups such as (poor) women and children and in ideologies of 'racial hygiene'.

Many of the social reforms carried out during the 1930s and early 1940s – together with the stabilisation of labour market relations and international economic developments – led to unprecedented economic growth and dramatic improvements in social conditions in post-war Sweden. This shift in social and economic conditions seems to be reflected in early post-war analysis of the family. Family policy was no longer targeted at population growth only; instead, social justice emerged as the dominant theme in the family policy discourse. Moreover, as is discussed in Chapter Three, an ambivalent family ideal dominated the period between 1940 and 1960. This ambivalence reflected a deepening of the work–family balance paradox from the 1930s; while family and social policy reforms supported the male-breadwinner model by enabling women to stay at home through initiatives such as universal maternity leave, government commissions proposed reforms such as state day care that encouraged mothers to enter the labour market.

While some experts legitimised women as the 'caring head' of the family, others stressed the dual roles of women, a discourse that reflected increasing female participation in the labour market.

By the end of the 1960s, the gap between policy regulations (based on a male-breadwinner ideal) and family life was becoming obvious; rising female labour market participation, increasing divorce rates and the expansion of social rights and benefits had changed the actual organisation of the family. Chapter Four is centred on the intellectual and political debate that led to the overhaul of family policy in the late 1960s and the 1970s. A sex-role debate, a radicalisation of the equality rhetoric within the labour movement and heightened labour market intervention on behalf of women were some of the ingredients of the political climate of the 1960s. The end result was a gender-neutral and gender-equal family ideal, and a radical breach with the male-breadwinner (and housewife) ideal of the post-war period.

During the 1960s, men were brought into the debate on gender equality and family policy, not least concerning the debate on parental leave. From then on, the conflict between family life and working life was officially defined as a concern for men as well as women. In addition, an increasing emphasis on children's need for their fathers marked a shift in the construction of fatherhood. An overarching political theme throughout this period was to produce incentives for women to become wage earners, and to create the necessary institutional underpinnings for this. Several major reforms resting on gender neutrality were enacted. At the same time, feminist research began to scrutinise and criticise gender equality policies; a new paradox emerged, based on feminist research showing that despite gender-neutral reforms and gender equality legislation, discrimination and gender segregation prevailed.

Chapter Five covers the period from the 1980s until the new millennium. This is a period marked by the complex interplay of deregulation of the Swedish model during the 1980s, a deep economic crisis in the early 1990s and the development of gender equality as a policy field, also embracing family policy. Gender equality policy as well as family policy came under heavy criticism in the 1980s. The main critics were feminists, who challenged dominant beliefs about gender equality, caring responsibilities and men's roles in the family. This transformation in the interpretation of gender relations coincided with the development of neoliberalism, embedded in a Swedish context and called circumscribed neoliberalism by some researchers.

In this context, family policy can be portrayed as shaped through two paradoxical paths: one that refers to defamiliarisation, individualisation and reflexive flexibility á la Giddens and Beck, and another where structural subordination of women is at the core of the analysis, following a particular strand in feminist research in Sweden. The resulting incoherence between defamiliarisation and structural explanations of female subordination shaped family policy paradoxes over this period.

Gender equality policies at the time had many different aspects, from equal representation in parliament to the inclusion of fathers in the gender equality project. Also, during the mid-1990s, the concept of gender mainstreaming came to the fore as gender equality ambitions were to permeate all political fields.

Chapter Six takes as its point of departure gender equality policy during the first decade of the new millennium, initially marked by the rise and fall of radical feminism in policy making, and later by the diversity turn in gender equality policy. The social democratic government lost in the election of 2006, and was succeeded by a centre-right (alliance) government. The alliance made individual freedom of choice its main point of departure, while recognising the existence of gender inequalities. This led the government to introduce family policy reforms aiming to facilitate women's entry into the labour market. The reforms introduced by the centre-right government can only be described as paradoxical. The (re)introduction of the cash-for-care-scheme directly contradicts the idea of full employment for all citizens. The other paradox lies in the ambition to enhance the freedom of choice for those individuals who are given incentives to participate in the labour market. However, the very foundation of gender equality (defined as a structural dimension) is still the dominant interpretation of the policy field. Thus, while the victory of the centre-right government in 2006 was an ideological watershed in some respects, some of the basic elements in Swedish family policy remained.

The seventh and final chapter draws together the findings of the preceding chapters, highlighting the reforms and visions that have shaped family policy paradoxes in Sweden over more than seven decades and have created the currently widely debated policy model for reconciling work and family life.

Notes

[1] Such a shift does not, however, necessarily entail shared responsibilities between women and men for unpaid work or, for that matter, for paid work. Women tend to work part time and maintain the responsibility for unpaid household work, at least in the Nordic context (Leira, 2002; Nyberg, 2002; Ahlberg et al, 2008).

[2] Yet other studies elucidate the origins of welfare systems, emphasising the often neglected role of female political mobilisation or 'maternalism' (Bock and Thane, 1991; Skocpol, 1992; Koven and Michels, 1993; Lewis, 1993; Orloff, 1996; Sainsbury, 2001).

[3] The debate about breadwinner models has reintroduced the notion of citizenship into social policy studies. In mainstream political studies, citizenship refers to individual rights and obligations, as well as inclusion and participation in political activities, but neglects the gender dimension (compare Siim, 2000). In 1985, Carol Pateman had already claimed that women were excluded from 'democratic citizenship' and active presence in political forums; their citizenship instead built on their experience of motherhood, citizenship via non-public life, in effect leading to a duality between public (male) and private (female) citizenship (Pateman, 1985, 1988; see also; Lister, 1997; Siim, 2000).

[4] This process has led to defamiliarisation, defined as 'the degree to which individual adults can uphold a socially acceptable standard of living, independently of family relationships, either through paid work or through social security provisions' (Lister, 1997, p 173). Arnlaug Leira defined the concept of familisation (or refamilisation) as 'policy measures that support parental care for children at home, and "defamilisation" for the public support of extra-family/extra-parental child-care, that is, for services provided by someone outside the family/household' (Leira, 2002, p 42).

TWO

Mapping, evaluating and formulating modern family life

The dire consequences of industrialisation triggered much debate over the 'social question', in Sweden as elsewhere. Poverty and unemployment were the two main issues debated in political and intellectual circles during the early decades of the 20th century, but they were not the only ones. Rescuing the family from the destructive effects of industrialisation was identified as the key to the long-term survival of society; saving the family from poverty, bad housing conditions and infant mortality, and upholding assumed morally correct sexual behaviour thus came to the forefront of debates. Perhaps the most debated issue concerned decreasing fertility rates, but women's participation in the labour market was also highlighted. Even though the dominant belief was that female employment threatened established family and gender norms, the divide between work and family life was obvious already in the early 1900s and became even clearer during the 1930s. This gave rise to the first family policy paradox: improving opportunities for married women in the labour market while encouraging childbirth and supporting stay-at-home wives. This chapter deals with how the concept of family was debated and interpreted in the very first steps towards a modern family policy.[1]

Gender relations in a male-breadwinner model

The growing numbers of women and children employed in industry in the early 1900s triggered the first steps towards legal protection for mothers in the workplace. Liberals, social democrats and even conservatives were taken aback by the social consequences of rising numbers of working women and children, and called for the protection of new mothers and children from heavy work. In 1900, parliament passed a law forbidding women and minors to work underground and preventing mothers from working at all during the first four weeks after giving birth (Carlsson, 1986; Wikander, 1999). A few years later, night work for women was banned. After that, the protection of working women came to a halt. Although government commissions suggested the introduction of 'motherhood support', 'breastfeeding support' and free midwifery services, these were never realised (Abukhanfusa, 1987). The turning point came in 1929, with the commission on motherhood protection (SOU 1929:28).

Up until then, the debate about female employment had fluctuated, primarily focusing on women's employment in industry and its psychological and physiological consequences. This was so despite the fact that most women were employed in farming and in service occupations, and that the proportion of women in industry was declining (Karlsson, 2001). The debate became increasingly fierce and the employment of women in industry became a major political concern. The fear of deteriorating moral standards triggered concerns about the break-up of the family, and even the social fabric as a whole, if the employment of women in industry were not halted (Carlsson, 1986; Karlsson, 2001, p 162).

The debate did not stop there. Even the earlier regulation of women's employment had been controversial. The ban on night work was vehemently opposed by female trade unionists as well as by social democratic and liberal feminists, who argued that a ban would hinder women from working rather than outlaw unhealthy employment (Carlsson, 1986). Such opposition was entirely ignored by the parliamentary majority – in which most social democrats participated, alongside conservatives and liberals – which acted on the conviction that women's employment threatened established gender relations and gender norms (Karlsson, 2001, p 164).

Meanwhile, with incomes rising for working-class and lower-middle-class families, the ideal of the single-earner household was gaining ground. For those families who achieved this ideal, the stay-at-home housewife signalled, according to the economic historian Lena Sommestad, 'a particularly advantageous solution to the main work-organisation problem of industrial society: the coordination of salaried employment outside the household with household work and child-care' (Sommestad, 2001, p 254). Consequently, women were framed as temporary participants in the labour market, leaving it after childbirth and returning only – if ever – after the children had grown up. It can therefore be argued that the prevailing view was that men were the wage earners and women the carers (Carlsson, 1986; Carlsson Wetterberg, 1992; Hirdman, 1998).

As argued earlier, seemingly perpetual unemployment in the 1930s triggered an intense debate on the social consequences of such stagnation. The issue was not only unemployment, but also social conditions in general – not least due to declining birth rates. This, it was argued, called for broad-based social reforms, which in their turn – if they were to be successful – had to be based on surveys of those conditions: How widespread was poverty? What did housing conditions for the urban working class look like? How could perinatal mortality be reduced? And how could fertility rates increase?

Population and family policy in the 1930s

When the social policy field expanded in the 1930s, family policy grew in importance as well. For the first time in modern history, a coherent family policy was emerging – as a proactive countermeasure to declining birth rates. An important role for the reinvigoration of social and family policy was the connection with contemporary social science.

Social policy reforms found inspiration primarily in descriptive social studies but also in contemporary sociological and social psychological theories. While the former offered rich sources of information, the latter gave templates for understanding the phenomena that had been documented within the empirical studies: how families were evolving, the consequences of the new division of labour for women and men, children's role in modern society, new patterns of sexual relations, birth rates and satisfaction within marriages, the evolution of motherhood and so on. An underlying theme was that of 'equality' as a goal for policy reforms to come.

Thus, the ideas debated during the 1930s mirror the complex and paradoxical relationship between the concepts of equality and difference. In theory, it was assumed that in an advanced society, all citizens should be equal. However, in practical politics and discussions, differences were emphasised in an effort to improve social conditions for selected groups, such as women and children, but also to put forward eugenic ideals. Family policy was then a paradoxical hybrid of egalitarianism, male breadwinning and eugenics, as discussed in the following sections.

Social science, family sociology and population trouble: starting points among experts and intellectuals

A scientific treatment of social policy has not yet been put on trial. But since social politics must be transformed into social planning, and since social planning must be carried out under rational control, and not just by fumbling policies, the time has come for social science scholars to step out of their isolation. In order to create social change, they must go beyond registration of facts and consistent analysing to put forward rational plans for special purposes. (Myrdal, 1944, p 20; author's translation)

These are the words of Alva Myrdal, the famous social democrat and intellectual. She challenged social scientists to contribute to the realisation of a progressive, science-based social policy. Scientific findings, Myrdal claimed, should form the foundation for social policy reforms. However, Alva Myrdal's exhortation illuminates a process that had already begun. A number of social reforms, as we will see, had already been initiated during the 1930s, mainly to reduce the widespread poverty, but also to tackle declining birth rates. The reforms were all based on government commission reports, studying social conditions and suggesting possible reforms to alleviate the social problems.

Social science then became an instrument in the attempts to improve social conditions. Inspired by contemporary social science theories, as well as empirical studies of social conditions, politicians and public intellectuals of the time described a society undergoing dramatic transformations. Agricultural employment was declining, while the industrial system was becoming larger and more complex by the day. And the impact was felt not least within families.

Contemporary family sociologists, such as William Fielding Ogburns, Ernest W. Burgess and Robert Lynd, had conducted studies of changing family forms and status, and their work influenced the lines of argument in several government commission reports on family policy in Sweden.

Family sociology had at the time developed in two main directions: interactionist and structural-functionalist. It was initially the former that became influential in Sweden, not least because of the influence on family policy of Alva Myrdal, who had been trained in this tradition in the US (Nilsson, 1994; Roman, 2004).

Within interactionist models, families were studied as a primary group, in which the members interact on the basis of their respective positions and roles. Increasingly, the interactionist models became the reference point for studies of problems and challenges within modern families, such as choice of spouse, adoption within marriage and divorce (Roman, 2004).

Eventually, the interactionist model was overshadowed in family policy debates by the newly fashionable structuralist-functionalist accounts of the family (Roman, 2004). Even with this change to the intellectual foundations of family policy, much remained the same. Families, it was argued among contemporary sociologists, had developed from the pre-modern model of the enlarged (cross-generational) family headed by the male patriarch to a modern nuclear family characterised by a more equal distribution of power and more egalitarian relations within the family – a 'democratic family' (Burgess and Locke, 1945). Swedish family policy readily absorbed these new intellectual tendencies, and the government commissions became a particularly important platform and forum for the emerging family ideals. The commissions pointed to the protracted transition between the models and the consequences that could be foreseen in the form of a crisis of the family. The male-breadwinner model emerged as the solution to this crisis.

The experts cited in the government commission reports argued that in pre-industrial society, families had been hierarchical but also decentred, as both women and men were engaged in work (SOU 1936:59; SOU 1938:13; SOU 1938:47). With industrialisation came the breakdown of this policy-centric family form; families became increasingly fractured according to the functional division characteristic of industrial society. Men's work was separated from the family sphere, with – the commissions claimed – drastic consequences for families (SOU 1938:47, p 52). After an initial period of turbulence and insecurity, families would adapt to the new conditions where gainful employment was concentrated on men and where domestic work was the domain of women (SOU 1938:47, p 53).

Most of the commission reports identified economic change as the prime mover behind changes in family structure in general, and the emergence of the male-breadwinner model in particular. Furthermore, the reports subscribed to these changes, underlining the new role of women as sole providers of care and as chiefly responsible for consumption. At the same time, the commissions acknowledged that the provision of care was evolving as well, with care increasingly being provided outside the home by public institutions. This included maternity care, education and to some extent childcare, even though kindergartens were still rare at the time. Added to this, there were lingering concerns about women (and children) who still participated in the labour market, and the pressures on dual-earner families (SOU 1936:59). Clearly, the male-breadwinner model was seen as more desirable than its dual-earner counterpart, not least from the point of view of the family.

The commissions also showed an interest in the more intimate relationships of modern families. One of the main challenges was related to sexuality. Previously, the commissions argued, the primary function of marriage was to make sexual relations legitimate. In recent years, the form and function of sexuality had become more differentiated and negotiated. Empirical studies also indicated that the existing 'marriage contract' did not appeal to all women, as in practice it often prevented them from participating in paid labour and higher education. Marriage tended to narrow the opportunities and outlooks for women, locking them into a cycle of child rearing and housekeeping. Interestingly, this was defined as dysfunctional, not only for women but also for society as a whole (SOU 1938:47).

The macro-sociological diagnosis thus made it clear that the rise of industrial society brought with it not only growing social division but also mounting tensions within the family, where women and men had become functionally separated from one another. This functional separation had an unexpected negative impact on the very survival of the family, as was evident in decreasing fertility levels. This, the commissions argued, called for urgent remedies, primarily within the broad realm of social policy. The first step in this direction was the establishment of a social housing commission, which laid the basis for the decision to support the construction of *barnrikehus* (houses with dwellings for low-income families with a large number of children), as well as support for poor families with many children (Olsson, 1992). When Alva Myrdal and Gunnar Myrdal published their widely discussed book *Crisis in the Population Question* (1934), they triggered an intense debate on the family and the future of fertility in Sweden (Hatje, 1974; Hirdman, 1989; Ohlander, 1992; Nilsson, 1994). Again, government commissions were active in the reorientation of family policy. The Population Commission, set up in 1935, published no less than 17 expert reports (written mainly by medical researchers and social scientists) covering a broad range of issues and resulting in several reforms, such as improved state support and job security for pregnant and postnatal women. Maternity wards were established to reduce infant mortality and ill health among pregnant women. Hospital deliveries were heavily subsidised and employers were no longer allowed to dismiss pregnant women or women with small children. The tax system was reformed to support families with children.[2] While some political disagreement still prevailed, the general political tone was consensual: family policy reforms were broadly supported.

One of the areas on which interest was focused was sexual habits. Studies of venereal disease and abortion indicated that sexual experience often preceded marriage, which was seen as a threat to satisfaction within marriage. Sexual habits thus became the next focus for the government commissions (SOU 1936:59; Hirdman, 1989; Elgán, 1994; Laskar, 2004).

On sexuality, reproduction and nuclear family ideals

When Swedish industrialisation took off in the 1880s, fertility had already begun to decline. From 1936, the government commission on sexuality studied the relationship between falling birth rates and changes in attitudes towards sexuality. The commission suspected that there might be such a correlation here, as other factors – the growing number of marriages and the stabilisation of the economy – had little impact on fertility levels. The commission explicitly pointed out a 'rationalisation of sexuality' as the dominant factor behind falling birth rates. It set out to study this 'rationalisation' and how it could be managed (SOU 1936:59, p 30 onwards).

The commission on sexuality related its work to that of several others carried out in this period, including the commissions on housing and motherhood. The commission on sexuality suggested that even the most intimate of social relations must be subject to political reform, in this case in the form of sexual health information provided by doctors, midwives, and primary and secondary school teachers, as well as through popular education, but it was also to be directed towards parents (SOU 1936:59, p 134). Focusing on venereal disease and contraceptives, sexual information was to provide for a more enlightened, and therefore in the long run a more productive, form of sexuality. In doing so, it widened the mandate for existing public organisations, in effect establishing a new layer of governance between the state and citizens. A striking aspect of this enlightening of sexuality was that it should be channelled through 'productive' and 'sustainable' families; not everybody was included and 'undesired' reproduction was to be limited (Elgán, 1994, p 154 onwards).

The stance towards pregnancy control was ambiguous. The commission expressed great concern over declining fertility levels, but also welcomed and even encouraged the use of contraceptives – for certain women within certain social groups, that is (SOU 1936:59, p 31). Blending social science and behavioural science with the then fashionable research on heredity hygiene, the commission argued that family formation could not be left entirely to individuals. Polemicising against those medical experts and political forces that opposed legal abortion, the commission pointed out certain instances where abortion was deemed to be suitable, for instance for women in poor health (including those with psychiatric disorders and those suffering from 'general weakness'), older women or 'worn-out mothers' (SOU 1936:59, p 49).[3] The commission explicitly referred to 'healthy women and children' as the cornerstones of viable families (SOU 1936:59, p 51).

Such values formed the basis of attempts to reform education, healthcare and indeed the family as an organisational entity. The commission reports and reform proposals had an almost Manichean view of the family, emphasising problematic concerns such as poverty, worn-out mothers and venereal diseases while pursuing the notion of a modern society peopled by healthy, strong citizens achieved through means such as sterilisation (Broberg and Roll-Hansen, 1996; Runcis, 1998; Tydén, 2002).

Declining fertility levels laid the foundation for a broad-based reorientation of family policy towards sexual habits, intimate relations, relations between parents and children and the balance between work and labour. On the basis of a 'grand narrative' of social modernisation, and the role of the family in it, the commissions made a wide variety of proposals. Two of the most significant areas of reform were support of pregnant and postnatal women and women's right to employment, two policy fields constituting one of the first modern family policy paradoxes. The ramifications were wide: how should women and men organise their lives, and how should they contribute to family incomes and well-being? How should the social and family policy of the future be devised? Which groups should, and should not, be targeted?

Protecting mothers and children

The question of how much responsibility society should take for pregnant women and women with newborn children has been the subject of debate among political parties and interest organisations throughout the 20th century and many solutions have been introduced over time.

Nevertheless, reforms aimed at supporting pregnant women and women with newborn children were debated for some time before anything actually happened. The commission report from 1929 on motherhood protection (SOU 1929:28), which laid the foundations for reformed maternity support, stressed both medical and social motives for a maternity insurance. Among the social motives, the commission singled out in particular the vulnerability of poor women in the labour market during and after pregnancy. The medical motives for a maternity insurance included the large number of difficult deliveries, high child mortality and women's physical and mental illness during and after childbirth.

Maternity insurance was eventually introduced in 1931. However, it was a relatively cumbersome system, where state subsidies to voluntary sickness funds were transformed into motherhood support. Such support, in its turn, covered the costs of deliveries and midwives' services, and included cash support for mothers. All female members of sickness insurance schemes were covered, while women with no such security were eligible for more meagre compensation (Bill 1931, no. 18).

There was still some distance to go to a general maternity insurance, but it had emerged as a principle – a basic citizen-based system, and a second-tier system based on membership of sickness insurance schemes. This duality came under increasing political fire, and again, and not for the last time, the government commission took on the role of trouble-shooter, this time in conjunction with the population commission.

In its report on childbirth care and midwifery, the population commission criticised the recently established maternity insurance, primarily for its residual coverage (SOU 1936:12). As a radical remedy, the commission suggested that the maternity insurance be made universal, a proposal that, as we shall see, was rejected by the social democratic government, which favoured an income-based system.

The population commission also called for a radical increase in state support for the care of mothers and children, in terms of both quality and quantity – it envisaged a universal, free system. A whole battery of proposals was presented, including initiatives to increase fertility levels and provide free state childbirth care and day care for working mothers (SOU 1936:15, p 47). Fashionable ideas about state day care appealed even to the more technical and practical government commissions, which had a political impact as the government later decided to go to parliament with a proposal to increase the level of maternity insurance and motherhood support.

Who should be covered? Universal or income-related reform policies

The commission proposals were thoroughly debated by government and met with resistance in parliament. The government made two related proposals: to establish needs-based motherhood support for low- and middle-income women, and a supplementary support scheme for women with 'urgent need of support' (Bill 1937, no. 38). The proposals as such did not meet with resistance, but the motivations behind them did: Who should be covered? How did motherhood support blend with the tradition of family autonomy? Should social insurance be citizenship-based or residual, be income-related or universal? These questions cut right through the ideological spectrum and haunted both the social democrats and their bourgeois contenders.

These questions coalesced in the issue of maternity support. While there were more specific issues at stake, such as the rights of pregnant and prenatal women, the broader issues pertained to the design of social and family policies in the future, and the possibility of achieving gender equality.

In the parliamentary debate, the positions were fixed: the social democrats – led by Gunnar Myrdal – argued in favour of a broad-based maternity insurance forming the central part of a general social insurance system rather than just residual support, while the centre-right opposition called for a means-tested insurance (AK protocol no. 29, 1937, and Ebon Andersson in the First Chamber). The social democrats, however, were not unanimous on the issue. Some, such as Myrdal, called for a more radical approach, where all (and not only the 92% who would in fact be covered by the insurance and support system) would be integrated to create a genuine universal system, while others, such as the Minister for Social Affairs, Gustav Möller, objected, arguing that visions and realities had to be aligned:

> When one suggests activities of this kind, one must avoid doing so in a way which triggers a successful reaction against social policy decisions taken in parliament. Large parts of the Swedish population

have difficulties in understanding why wealthy people should receive
support from the state, even if it is a form of child support, that is, with
population-policy motives. (FK protocol no. 29, 1937, p 10)

An income limit would ensure, Möller argued, that state support targeted only
families in real need of support. Similar arguments were raised by for example the
liberals in the Second Chamber of the Swedish parliament, where it was argued
that resource scarcity called for a more restrictive stance, directing state support
primarily to those 'truly in need' (Ivar Österström, AK protocol no. 29, 1937, p
10). Gunnar Myrdal opposed Möller's stance, and argued that universal support
would indeed primarily benefit those in need, even though it also covered those
with a secured economic position (FK protocol no. 29, 1937, p 16). Referring
to international developments, in particular fascist and Nazi policies in Italy and
Germany, Myrdal argued that the most successful population policies were to be
found in 'solid democracies' like the US and France. There, successful attempts
had been made to eradicate the psychological, economic and social obstacles
to increased fertility – an experience and a policy model that Sweden should
emulate, Myrdal argued.

An outlier in the debate was the Agrarian Party, represented by Nils Wohlin, a
professor of statistics and Director-General of the Swedish Customs Authority.
Wohlin, who had a predilection for eugenics, concurred with the commission's
proposal to establish a universal system, but for reasons quite different from those
of Myrdal. For Wohlin, the proposal primarily elevated motherhood, thereby
securing the future of the nation. Furthermore, universal reforms repressed class
conflicts and united the nation, Wohlin claimed:

> It may be of some future importance to take advantage of the backing
> of all classes for the reform policy that we aim to and must pursue.
> I believe that there will come a day when we, in this country, have
> eschewed the old class-political ideas and view issues like these in a
> broader, national context. (FK protocol no. 29, 1937, p 24)

If universal coverage was one dividing issue, the status of working women was
another, and one that intersected with universalism. The social democrat Olivia
Nordgren pointed to women employed in industry, who were not allowed to
work immediately after childbirth, arguing that a two-tier system (comprising
universal maternity insurance and means-tested additional maternity support)
stigmatised these women as 'particularly needy'. However, her suggested remedy
was not a universal integrated maternity support system (à la Gunnar Myrdal) but
a two-tier, means-tested model (AK protocol no. 29, 1937, pp 14-15).

In general, the social democrats eschewed a universal system, claiming that
targeting and precision were far more important than inclusion. Indeed, a universal
maternity insurance was seen by one social democrat as a goal primarily for non-

working, well-to-do women who prided themselves on earning some money on their own (AK protocol no. 29, 1937, p 27).

The proposal to establish a means-tested maternity insurance was passed easily, with a majority in both chambers. Those who had argued for a universal model had to recognise defeat for the time being. The new system had three elements: means-tested maternity support; motherhood support tied to membership of sickness insurance funds; and a means-tested motherhood allowance designed to complement motherhood support.

Alongside the debate on the form and function of maternity insurance, the issue of married women's status in the labour market continued to be a source of political strife. The debates gravitated between two paradoxical positions – women as carers and women as participants in the labour market. Both positions revolve around issues of family constitution and gender equality, and, more generally, the interaction between family life and paid employment.

Married women's right to work

Married women's right to work was a contested issue in the 1930s. On the one hand, women's organisations flourished; they gained their own political voice and published their own magazines, in which they articulated a vision of womanhood that combined the roles of both child-rearer and employee. On the other hand, the centre-right parties in particular strongly opposed the idea that married women could be employed by the state or by the municipalities (Frangeur, 1998, p 244).

Again, the task of reconciling these contrasting views fell on the government commissions. As the issues at stake concerned the population as a whole, the population commission again became the vehicle for conflict resolution and policy articulation.

The question was primarily how married women could combine the roles of mother and participant in the labour market. In one sense, the issue was reactive, as more and more women were joining the labour market, but it also led to the creation of other interested parties with labour market expertise, including a women's work committee appointed by the Ministry of Finance in 1935 that scrutinised issues such as wage formation, unemployment and the demand for male and female labour. However, as the key ministry for population policy and as the head of the ubiquitous population commission, the Ministry for Social Affairs also had a stake in this area, and began to consider issues such as conditions for pregnant and postnatal women.

Hence, while experts and government commissions figured prominently in the debates on female labour, there were several different sources and forms of expertise in operation. While there were some interaction between the population commission and the Ministry of Finance/women's work committee, and some experts worked for both, their mandates and their orientation towards family policy were radically different.

The population commission proposal

Most of the formal obstacles to female employment had been eradicated by the mid-1930s. Some restrictions remained, such as a law from 1912 that forbade women to work just before childbirth and for four weeks afterwards. Another, more controversial issue concerned the right of employers to dismiss pregnant, engaged or married women, primarily used in the service sector (banking, insurance and trade). Public sector employers did not exercise this right, and the difference between the practices of private and public sector employers became an issue for the government commissions.

The population commission presented a report on the legal status of working women in 1938 (SOU 1938:13), which proposed that the practice of dismissing pregnant, engaged or married women should not be permitted. The proposal was part of the population policy debate on measures to stop decreasing fertility, and indicated that malign legal treatment of women hindered the combination of employment and family formation (SOU 1938:13, p 19).

The commission argued that legal obstacles to female employment had no place in modern societies. If women could retain their employment after marrying, they would also be more willing to have children: 'If one diminishes the possibilities to work only in connection with childbirth, one creates a strong motive for an extreme form of family planning' (SOU 1938:13, p 12). There was a direct connection between the legal situation and population policy; allowing dismissals of married women and women with children was not only distant from reality but also antisocial, as it actually hindered people from getting married and encouraged premarital relations and illegal abortions (SOU 1938:13, p 20).

What the population commission proposed was therefore nothing less than a dual-earner family, dismissing the male-breadwinner model as counterproductive in a 'modern society'. While its motives were related less to gender equality per se than to population policy, the commission articulated a sharp critique of the notion of women as dependent on men. Women, including those who were married and with children, should instead be encouraged to take part in the labour market. Hence, the commission proposed that dismissals of pregnant or married women must be outlawed; instead, the positions of pregnant and postnatal women should be strengthened through the reinforced maternity insurance scheme. While in practice the proposals targeted women, they also pertained to men (SOU 1938:13, p 29); theoretically, then, men were covered by the proposed legislation. Thus, as early as the 1930s, the commission had proposed a gender-neutral law, albeit indirectly.

The commission's proposal attracted some criticism, however; two of its own conservative members protested by writing reservations in the report itself. In particular, they opposed the idea of forbidding employers to dismiss pregnant women, but they were also critical of the notion that only pregnant and postnatal women in paid employment should benefit from the enhanced maternity insurance – such a limitation, the argument went, did not take account of pregnant women who were doing unpaid work in the home.

The women's work committee proposal

The women's work committee also presented its report in 1938 (SOU 1938:47). Against the background of the economic crisis of the 1930s and the enactment of new legislation pertaining to women (universal suffrage, a new marriage Act and a new Act on female public sector employment), the time was now ripe for a reform of labour market regulation (SOU 1938:47, p 7 onwards). However, a law that had yet to be enacted was one that prevented employers from dismissing pregnant or married women. The commission started out by asserting that the gendered division of labour was not related to biological differences, as women 'neither from a physical nor a psychological perspective are different in such a way that one or the other of the genders is totally superior' (SOU 1938:47, p 45).

Backing its argument with the research of the family sociologist William Ogburn, the commission instead highlighted the social factors behind the gender division in the labour market, motherhood being the most important. With industrialisation, the commission argued, productive work had migrated from the household to the market, and as motherhood tied women to the household, a gendered labour market naturally ensued. But motherhood was not the only factor at play. Economic conditions within industrial society had been transformed when paid labour was divorced from household work. As a result, the social constitution of the family had been transformed. Aligning itself with the discourse of topical sociological theories of the time, the commission located these changes in its reproductive, educational and personal-affective functions.

However, the key to the gender division of labour was the household: 'Among the conditions that ultimately affect division of labour as well as wage differentials between women and men, women's closer connection to the family stands out' of which the strongest expression was the 'for long most common form of work for women, namely household work' (SOU 1938:47, pp 64-5).

The commission outlined a broad reform agenda for increasing gender equality in the labour market, improving working conditions for women (Frangeur, 1998). However, it did not propose legislation preventing employers from dismissing women when they become pregnant or marry. This, the commission argued, should be voluntary, but it also recognised the problems women faced when they entered the labour market.

In a historically grounded analysis of labour market evolution, the commission argued that changes in labour market conditions must go hand in hand with a transformation of gender relations within the family. As more women entered the labour market, they had the double burden of responsibilities both at home and at work: 'What is primarily needed is a change of the demands traditionally put on women for caring and household organisation. The more *equal* women and men become in relation to paid labour, the less women should be expected to be at the disposal of other family members' (SOU 1938:47, p 336, emphasis added).

This, the commission conceded, was an urgent task. In the absence of legislation, it put forward several suggestions for alleviating the burden for women (and men). The right to work part time was one proposal, and the right to return to the same type of work after pregnancy and childbirth another. The commission also suggested that women have the right to retain their given name after marriage (aimed particularly at women who had established themselves with firms and businesses carrying their parents' family name), and put forward proposals for investments in state day care and state subsidies for household work, even though it recognised that increased gender equality and the rationalisation of housework were the best ways of supporting families (SOU 1938:47).

Debating married women's work

Two government commissions (SOU 1938:47; SOU 1938:13) had, by 1938, made different, but largely overlapping, proposals for improving conditions for working women. One suggested a prohibition of employers' dismissals of married, engaged or pregnant women, while the other took a more cautious stance, suggesting voluntary measures instead. The decision on which way to go was therefore left to government and ultimately parliament.

The government preferred the legal approach and sided with the population commission. Aside from an exception for small firms with three employees or less, it proposed that all employers be prohibited from dismissing women on the grounds of marriage, engagement, pregnancy or childbirth.

The proposal was debated in parliament in May 1939, and the government Bill was supported in both chambers. With effect from 1 July 1939, it was no longer legal for employers to dismiss women on the grounds of engagement, marriage, pregnancy or childbirth. The way the proposal was received in the parliamentary debates, however, illustrates rather neatly the political positions on female work at the time.

In the debates, there were clear differences of opinion, as well as some agreement, between the political factions. Several female parliament members from the bourgeois parties were in favour of legislation, and there was general agreement on the core issue, namely the prohibition on employers to dismiss engaged, married or pregnant women. The disputes concerned the legal aspects of the proposal, which the Conservative Party in particular opposed. Its line of argument was fourfold. First, by enforcing employment standards by law, the proposal broke with the central premise of the existing labour market agreement (the Saltsjöbaden Agreement). Second, as the proposed legislation was universal and did not distinguish pregnant single women from married women, it challenged the hegemony and moral superiority of the family. Third, it threatened the profitability of firms, as they would be unable to dismiss workers with dual loyalties (family and work), which would result in lower productivity. Fourth, it would discriminate against women in the labour market, as many employers would avoid hiring women or dismiss them *before* they became pregnant or married (FK protocol no. 27, 1939). Another argument against the legislation was that it actually hindered younger women from establishing themselves in the labour market, as married women more prone and suited to returning to household work were locked into gainful employment (AK protocol no. 27, 1939, p 47).

If the Conservative Party was critical of the proposed legislation, and identified some structural advantages of the employers' practices, the other bourgeois parties had a more ambiguous stance. Even the Conservative Party was divided internally, particularly where those members of parliament engaged in population policy viewed legislation as a necessary step to boost fertility. The Agrarian Party, for instance, sided with the government on the issue, citing the connection between labour legislation and fertility (the latter being the party's overriding concern). One member of parliament, Nils Wohlin, argued that given the pressing need for radical population policy measures, it was not enough to wait for employers to take voluntary action.

The criticism from the far left, the Communist Party, was that the proposal did not go far enough and that it left gender relations intact; in contemporary society, families were increasingly dependent on not just one but two incomes, and the male-breadwinner model was deemed obsolete. In particular, the critique was aimed at the impact of gender inequalities on fertility levels and the number of illegal abortions. The double standards of the patriarchal societies were left to women to resolve, with disastrous consequences:

> Society calls for more children, but the same society dictates: you are a woman, it is you who carry the next generation, but as a woman your salary is lower! You are dismissed if you marry or give birth. You are punished if you take away your baby. You must be moral and live in a legal marriage, but you are not allowed to work. Give society children! (AK protocol no. 27, 1939, p 51)

Of particular criticism was the exception for small firms, but there was also disapproval over the general tone of the debate, which seemed to indicate that there was competition between qualified women and men in the labour market (where men dominated), while, in reality, their fates were intertwined with the preservation of the family and, in the long run, of society itself.

The social democratic government, headed by Prime Minister Per Albin Hansson, acknowledged the wide-ranging critique of employers' practices from all political factions. The question that remained was how to proceed, and whether the solution should encompass legislation or voluntary agreements. Responding to Hansson's (rhetorical) question, Minister for Social Affairs Forslund argued that promises made on the basis of voluntary agreements did not hold water, at least not in this area. The relationship between employers and employees was simply too uneven and hierarchical. The Saltsjöbaden Agreement did not falsify this view, Forslund argued, as it did not deal with labour conditions but rather the framework conditions for labour peace and industrial relations. Furthermore, as women already enjoyed some employment protection in the public sector, it was only seen as natural to extend it to the private sector, even by fiat. Indeed, the proposed legislation was seen as a forerunner of a more comprehensive redressing of power relations in the labour market: 'When I hear [Conservative MP] Wistrand speak ... I am reminded of the desire to retain a system where "I and no one else should decide"' (FK protocol no. 27, 1939, p 25).

The Minister for Trade, and former Minister for Social Affairs, Gustav Möller, made two contributions to the debate. First, he claimed that the time was ripe for legislation; neither further inquiries nor voluntary agreements were sufficient, as the issue of employers' practices in relation to married or pregnant women was pressing. Second, legislation reflected structural changes in the labour market, as it would primarily be the growing number of women employed as clerks or working in the service sector that would be covered, while very few women in working in industry were affected by the employers' dismissal practices (FK protocol no. 27, 1939, p 33). Hence, reflecting the social democratic stance towards the maternity insurance scheme, and indicative of future social policy initiatives, Möller favoured reforms that targeted cross-class constituencies rather than the working class alone. However – and in this he sided with liberal members of parliament such as Kerstin Hesselgren (a member of the women's work committee established by the Ministry of finance) – he took a cautious stance towards legislation, and remained committed to broad-based, popularly anchored reforms (AK protocol no. 27, 1939, p 35).

In both chambers of parliament, then, there was consensus about the principle of dismissing women when they married, got engaged or became pregnant. Many members, however, questioned whether legislation was the best way to handle the issue, and many interesting views were expressed about the treatment of women in the labour market and whether women should participate in paid employment at all after marrying. Traditional views were confronted with modern ones, and this was reflected in the opinions expressed. But the question of married women's entitlement to paid employment also encompassed the complex issue of how the social policy reforms were to be implemented. Was it best to proceed slowly, as Möller and Hesselgren advocated? Or should the process be accelerated, thus running the risk of provoking opinion that might not perhaps always be favourably disposed to the proposals?

Conclusion

Gender, work and welfare

Early 20th-century Sweden was marked by a combination of rapid urbanisation, deep social divisions, high unemployment in a turbulent labour market, decreasing fertility rates and generally unstable political conditions. In this time of social and economic turmoil, various initiatives were taken to stabilise social conditions and encourage a rise in fertility levels (Myrdal and Myrdal, 1934). While much of the change was discursive, a string of social reforms ensued in the 1930s, such as the introduction of antenatal clinics and child welfare centres, legal prohibition of the dismissal of married or pregnant women from the workplace and means-tested maternity support.

These reforms reflected the intertwining of social forces and government policy making, and many of them originated in recommendations based on government commission reports on social conditions. These reports portrayed the family as a unit going through a period of crisis, mainly as a result of industrialisation, resulting in declining birth rates. A major reason for this crisis, it was argued, was the new division of labour, whereby men were isolated from the household and from women and children. The traditional concept of the family was subject to new ideas about how to organise the household and there was a gradual move towards the single-earner model. Following Jane Lewis's terminology, by the 1930s Sweden was experiencing the emergence of the male-breadwinner model, with few women in the labour force as a result of poorly developed childcare services and a bias in the social insurance and the taxation systems against dual-earner families.

Ideas about universal welfare systems were gradually emerging in the political discourse of the 1930s. At the time, individual livelihood was dependent on market performance. However, the ideological landscape was slowly changing, and some actors within the Social Democratic, Liberal and Agrarian Parties argued for population-based social policy, even though their ideological motives and ultimate goals differed. Even if it is premature to speak about a welfare state in the 1930s, the idea of the 'People's Home' had been articulated as a distinctive feature of Swedish society by Per-Albin Hansson and other leading social democrats. The parliamentary debates on maternity insurance are one example of where these ideas were articulated. However, there was still an outspoken fear of the costs and social consequences of universal support, not least within the social democratic government, which lead to a temporary defeat for the demands for universal rights.

Gender, care and welfare

In this period, equality between women and men – within the family, in the home and in the labour market – were constructed as a means of achieving social democracy. In radical assumptions about the future of modern society and the new family, women would be released from their duties as carers, mainly by shifting the responsibility for childcare on to society.

However, the reality, in terms of population and family policy reforms, was less radical. Many of the proposals merely resulted in new family policy paradoxes, apparent, for example, in initiatives aimed to encourage women to have more children at the same time as entering the workplace. Even if attempts to manage the complex relationship between paid work and (unpaid) family life were being articulated during the 1930s, they ultimately failed as they only targeted women, leaving men's position in the labour market untouched.

In this context, the concept of care becomes essential in understanding the relationship between public and private, or paid and unpaid, work (Daly and Lewis, 2000). Even if radical ideas about women's position in society were advanced at the time, the dominant ideology emphasised women as carers and loving mothers. Women (with small children) were relegated to the position of caretakers, for households, men and children. The new maternity insurance system was instrumental in this respect. The debates on the employment rights of married women coincided with these views. The recurrent theme was how women could combine paid and unpaid (family) work, while the issue of men participating in the unpaid domain and sharing household responsibilities with women was never raised. The way to release women from unpaid labour to participate in the labour market on equal terms with men, it was argued, was through the provision of state day care, not by including men in the domain of family work, although neither argument was not to occur in the period covered in this chapter.

(Gender) equality in the 1930s

Even if visions about gender equality existed in both political and academic discourses at the time, social reforms were mainly directed towards women. Thus, gender equality was aligned with women's role in society, since men's position in the labour market never was questioned or targeted in family policy debates. Equality as a concept was instead directed towards improving the conditions of the working class.

Alongside the rise of egalitarian ideals, discussions on eugenics took off. Here, government commissions played an avant-garde role, not stopping at abortion as a method of birth control. By referring to the debate on eugenics in contemporary medical, psychological and sociological research, some commissions argued that women (and later men) suffering from psychological and neurological diseases should be excluded from the possibility of having children. The idea of using sterilisation as a method of birth control was thereby introduced, and later implemented in the practical politics of all Nordic countries and other European countries.

This reflects the complex relationship between the concepts of equality and difference. Equality was used as an ideological catchword; in theory, it was assumed that in modern society all citizens would be equal. However, in practice, differences were emphasised in the pursuit of improved social conditions, which paved the way for ideals of racial hygiene.

Population and family policy as it developed during the 1930s thus became a paradoxical combination of egalitarianism, male-breadwinner focus and eugenic ideals, not easily blended into a coherent policy mix but rather representing different approaches to the family and to the concept of 'equality'. Some of these ideals followed the making of family policy reforms into the post-war period, although family policy reforms did not run smoothly.

Notes

[1] Several steps towards the 'modernisation' of family relations had already been taken, such as the reformation of the Marriage Act during the 1920s (see Melby et al, 2006).

[2] People did not speak in terms of family policy reforms in the 1930s, although the phrase 'family-preserving policy' (*familjevårdande politik*) does occur in parliamentary debates as a way of distinguishing the population question from other issues. This family-preserving policy contained many elements, such as the design of maternity insurance and the organisation of obstetric care and maternity and childcare, as well as housing and certain tax matters. See also Ann-Sofie Ohlander, who argues that family policy became an established term at the end of the 1940s (Ohlander, 1992, p 215 onwards).

[3] Sterilisation was introduced in 1934 as a means of limiting 'undesirable' groups.

THREE

The family in the Swedish model

The welfare institutions that were established in post-war Sweden had counterparts elsewhere in Europe, and the ideas behind the welfare policies were primarily imported from elsewhere. The Beveridge Report, which shaped many debates and policy practices in the immediate post-war, is a case in point (Beveridge, 1942). As time went on, international policy trends filtered down into national institutional and political trajectories. One such trajectory was the Swedish model and the template for conflict resolution that had been devised in the 1938 Saltsjöbaden Agreement, which was complemented and sustained by an active labour market policy, social insurance and, later, the expansion of social services.

A centrepiece in the post-war welfare 'harvest time' was family support. Beginning in the 1930s with housing policy measures, improved standards in healthcare for mothers and children and measures to reduce insecurity for women in the labour market, ambitions grew in the 1940s, accompanied by a significant change in social policy discourse. While 1930s social policy was embedded in population policy, the link between the two weakened after the war. Instead, a new discourse and policy practice replaced population policy and its various sub-policies targeting fertility levels. Instead, social policy measures were framed in terms of justice and equality. This was a harbinger of a new welfare era.

This did not mean that the new welfare model emerged without friction. Supporting families with children is a case in point, as the evolution of family policy was torn between two strong and, as argued in the previous chapter, paradoxical forces in Swedish politics – securing the role of women in the labour market while simultaneously improving housewives' standing and situation. In effect, Sweden was now experiencing the battle between two family policy paradigms: the dual-income model and the male-breadwinner model.

Hence, the debate focused on the role of women in the household and in the labour market, sparked off by the book *Women's Two Roles* by Alva Myrdal and her British colleague Viola Klein (Klein and Myrdal, 1957). They highlighted the family policy paradox: the male-breadwinner–female-housewife ideal on the one hand and the desire to improve working conditions for employed women on the other. The paradox showed not only in the ideological deliberations, but also in policy practice. Two policy ideals coexisted, one that targeted housewives and family relations and another that connected working women with labour market and social policy reforms, to improve women's capacity to balance the often ambivalent and contradictory demands of working life and family care (Hatje, 1999, p 233 onwards). The first policy strand took the family and its preservation in changing social conditions as its starting point, while the other was formulated in a different policy context in which economic growth and labour market dynamics shaped the discourse and practice. The latter became increasingly important with the emergence of a model for combining high growth, low unemployment and limited inflation.

Institutionalising the Swedish model

The political discourse of the 1950s was ambitious: full employment, high growth, low inflation and improved social conditions, all at the same time. To align all these seemingly incompatible goals, a combination of economic policy measures was established, including a stringent financial policy and activist labour market regulation (known as the Rehn-Meidner model)[1], which – against the background of stable and peaceful relations between unions and employers (following the 1938 Saltsjöbaden Agreement) and unprecedented growth in the public sector – has been termed 'the Swedish model' (Misgeld et al, 1992; Rothstein, 1992, 1996; Rehnberg, 1999).[2]

This model did not emerge effortlessly. When the wartime grand coalition stepped down, it was succeeded by a social democratic minority government. In its post-war programme, the Social Democratic Party suggested several far-reaching proposals to increase political influence on the Swedish economy. This, together with comprehensive tax reforms in 1947, led to a massive ideological confrontation between the social democrats and the bourgeois opposition, and the employers sided with the centre-right parties (Lewin, 1967). However, the tensions ebbed away after the failure of the bourgeois parties to oust the social democratic government in the 1948 election. The social democrats, for their part, toned down their ambitions to steer the economy, and instead ventured into reforms of social policy and labour market policy (Olsson, 1992).

The outbreak of the Korean War in 1950 increased the price of raw materials, fuel and shipping. This propelled economic growth in Sweden, as Swedish export prices experienced a 74% rise, while import process rose by only 39%. Surprisingly, the Korean boom was not succeeded by an economic downswing; instead, it marked the beginning of a phase of uninterrupted growth for another 25 years (Matthiessen, 1970; Benner, 1997; Schön, 2000). On average, the economy grew by some 4% between 1950 and 1974, after-tax wages doubled and consumption skyrocketed. The economic expansion was primarily borne by industry, and industrial employment peaked in the mid-1960s at over 50% of total employment (Olsson, 1996).

Even though the ideological reorientation announced in the post-war programme came to naught, several of the ideas behind it survived. In particular, the late 1940s saw the first steps towards the institutionalisation of perhaps the most important element in the post-war policy mix: an active labour market policy that in turn came to affect family policy development. In two reports, the government commission on wartime economic planning outlined a new stance on unemployment, including mobility support, improved vocational training, investments in schooling and better instruments for planning and predicting labour market trends (SOU 1945:36; SOU 1947:24). In the ensuing government Bill, it was proposed to establish a permanent body for labour market policy, the National Labour Market Board (AMS). Its first Director-General, Gustav Vahlund, was recruited from the Swedish Trade Union Confederation, LO. Vahlund also chaired the group within LO that wrote an influential report, *Fackföreningsrörelsen och den fulla sysselsättningen* (*The Trade Union Movement and Full Employment*), which outlined the post-war economic programme (LO, 1951).

The main authors of the 1951 report were the LO economists Gösta Rehn and Rudolf Meidner. They codified an emerging practice on the Swedish labour market, where rationalisations were welcomed, even at the cost of lost jobs. For full employment to be achieved, inefficient working methods, companies and even whole sectors had to be squeezed out. In doing so, poor working conditions in low-paid jobs within unprofitable firms and industries were phased out and more profitable and well-organised sectors and industries could benefit from the resulting stable supply of labour. This not only provided profitable and secure jobs, but also reduced the inflationary bottlenecks caused by a labour market operating at very high capacity.

A critical element behind this development model was the centralisation of wage bargaining, which began between the major trade union and employers' organisations, LO and SAF (the Swedish Employers' Federation) in 1956. The main aim was to secure a supply of labour for expanding regions and sectors, thereby institutionalising full employment without inflation. The idea was to secure and offer the whole population economic and social security while fostering economic growth through full employment. However, full employment at the time was aimed at men only, with women as dependents or employed part time (Hirdman, 1998; Lundqvist, 2007).

Labour market policy was the cornerstone of the post-war socioeconomic model. Social policy was another core element, primarily as a redistributive means in an era of seemingly uninterrupted economic growth. However, social policy also had a productivist undertone, as all major social policy reforms after 1948 (when two universal programmes, for child allowance and basic pensions, had been installed) were based on the so-called income replacement principle, which safeguarded previously earned incomes in case of unemployment, poor health, pregnancy and childbirth (Olsson, 1992).

Family policy slowly became a part of this harvest period in Swedish politics. The family remained a critical and sensitive issue; should it be left to its own devices or should the state intervene in a more comprehensive way to support families with children and to balance the paradoxical demands of unpaid care and gainful employment?

Family policy expansion

When fertility levels, which had grown in the late 1930s, began to decline again in the early 1940s, the government responded by appointing a new population policy commission. Together with two other government commissions (the commission for social care and the housing policy commission), it took a special interest in conditions for families with children and made several proposals to improve economic conditions. One of its most discussed ideas, first formulated in a report from 1946, *Betänkande om barnkostnadernas fördelning. Med förslag angående allmänna barnbidrag m.m.* (SOU 1946:5), was to introduce universal child allowances.

The report was written by a group of government-appointed experts, chaired by the then Minister of Social Affairs, Tage Erlander (who later became prime minister). The report concluded that economic redistribution had not reached far enough and needed to be sharpened, to improve the social standing of families with children. A three-pronged strategy was devised, based on motives of fertility, justice and redistribution. The fertility motives related social reforms to population growth, and in particular its qualitative aspects (which children were born in which social circumstances) (SOU 1946:5, pp 18-19). The motive pertaining to justice was that families with children should not be disadvantaged compared with those without children, and that the cost of children should as far as possible be carried by the state. The social redistributive motives pointed to the need to guarantee all children a basic level of security (SOU 1946:5, p 21).

The commission made it clear that having children was costly, as the wartime experience of price increases had made painfully clear. If fertility levels were to rise, the willingness of women and men to have children must be stimulated by means of a much more ambitious social policy. If increasing costs related to growing families were not matched by income growth, the end result would be a negative dynamic of insecurity and declining fertility levels. The pressure was particularly felt by the growing industrial class.

With growing numbers of women entering the labour market, and with no adjustments in the organisation of household work, a double burden on women would ensue. To improve conditions for working women, it was suggested that the responsibility for housework should be shared, not between women and men but between women and the state (SOU 1946:5, p 53). Increased cash support for families (housing support, economic support during pregnancy and contributions to schoolchildren's clothing) was therefore only one facet of family support; the other was more widespread access to social services. As far as cash support was concerned, the commissions suggested a reorientation (and relabelling) towards consumption-enhancing support rather than, as was the practice at the time, in-kind support. The instrumental motive was central, as the idea was to share the cost of children, 'on the one hand to integrate support into the family income, and on the other hand to connect the purchasing power to the capacity of Swedish industry' (SOU 1946:5, p 58).

Translating these rather general ambitions into practical policy was another matter, which included public loans to support newly married couples for housing and for extra costs in relation to pregnancy and childbirth (a system established back in 1938). Maternity support was enlarged and expanded (SOU 1946:23), as were healthcare for children and measures to prevent abortions. The commissions also considered raising the slim state subsidies to day-care centres and kindergartens (SOU 1943:9).

In-kind support was still considered an appropriate family policy instrument (although it would soon cease) and targeted in particular food and nutrition. Given the nutritional deficiencies among families with children, a system of cash benefits for purchasing milk, cheese, red meat, pork, eggs, fruit and vegetables was proposed, to enhance the nutrition levels of Swedish youth and to support the Swedish food industry. Families with children were also to be eligible for support for the purchase of clothing and shoes, the parallel motive behind this measure being to 'stimulate the standardisation of production in the area' (SOU 1946:5, p 165).

Finally, the commission proposed the introduction of general child allowances for all children up to the age of 16 irrespective of social background or geographical location (SOU 1946:5, p 287). This, together with all the previously mentioned support schemes (cash benefits, in-kind support and improved childcare services), formed the discursive thrust of the family policy drive of the immediate post-war period.

Introducing child allowance

In 1947, the Minister for Social Affairs Gustav Möller presented government Bill no. 220 on child allowances. The sum of 260 kronor per year would go directly to the mother (only if mothers were absent or otherwise 'hindered from caretaking' would fathers benefit). Building on the report from the population commission, but only picking up its proposal on child allowances, Möller claimed that much had changed in the last decade; almost all pregnant and postnatal women were covered by maternity insurance or motherhood support, the provision of housing for large families had expanded rapidly, which had narrowed the income gap between families with and without children, and hospital-based obstetric services had proliferated.

Despite their background in population policy, the reforms mentioned by Möller were slowly integrated into a new policy discourse of redistribution and social justice. Furthermore, and perhaps even more significantly, they were aligned with labour market policy. As labour shortages were becoming salient in the late 1940s, increasing female labour market participation was seen as necessary to reduce the shortage of labour. Even at this early stage, family policy was deeply embedded in labour market regulation, a pattern that has stuck: 'Labour market conditions can pull women, who otherwise would have been occupied with housekeeping, to enter the labour market. These tendencies will lead to considerable difficulties and constraints for families' (Bill 1947, no. 220, p 18).

Family policy therefore emerged against the backdrop of an unstable relationship between paid labour and household work. The policy outline was indeed very complex, as it spanned gender roles, family relations, labour market conditions and the preconditions for economic growth. Thus, from very early on, family policy was integrated with economic growth and employment.

A first step towards a universal social policy system

The government proposal was to establish universal child allowances. Means-tested child allowances were rejected, mainly because they would create an overblown bureaucracy. Instead, child allowances acted as a flat-rate payment to which other support schemes could be added, both universal and means-tested (Bill 1947, no. 220, p 52).

   Like other family policy issues, the concept of child allowances did not cause any major friction between the political parties, but, again, the conservatives were outliers in the debate, arguing for a differentiated, means-tested system. The conservatives preferred in-kind support to cash payments, purportedly for reasons of justice and efficiency.[3] However, some of the most enthusiastic proponents of universal, cash-based child allowances came from the other bourgeois parties. The ubiquitous Nils Wahlund of the Agrarian Party celebrated the proposal as an 'icebreaker' for a 'social family policy' (AK protocol no. 35, 1947, p 186). Wahlund was particularly content with the broad-based support of a universal child allowance system:

> I do not want the child allowances to be seen as a kind of gift from society, but as an honestly deserved support of Sweden's mothers for securing future generations by giving birth to and raising children – or, putting it in plain language, for securing the future needs for labour. Therefore it is only fair that the child allowances should be equal for all. (AK protocol no. 35, 1947, p 187)

The government proposal passed easily through parliament, and on 1 January 1948 the new system was established. This was the first universal, cash-based welfare programme in Sweden and it shaped the path for future welfare reforms. Another important aspect of the decision was its connection between family policy and labour market regulation. In the preparations for the reform, it was explicitly mentioned that the relationship between household work and gainful employment had to be adjusted if women were to enter the labour market. However, adding to the paradox and complexity of family policy, other government experts and commissions had a different focus on the family, emphasising its role as a nurturing and stabilising institution in society.

Producing care, security and welfare

Among its many tasks, the population commission in 1941 was asked to analyse the results of previous family policy reforms as well the organisation of the family.

It presented a report on homes and families in 1947, with the aim of analysing social changes affecting the 'internal organisation' of families (SOU 1947:46, p 6).

The report went on to criticise the now-established understanding of social change (with industrialisation leading to urbanisation, mobility and division of labour, including the separation between work and home life), or at least its tone of determinism. It highlighted its neglected and negative aspects, including the stress it put on the family, 'the most stable and most important group for humans' (SOU 1947:46, p 12), and argued instead for the naturalisation of social change. Backing its arguments in the interactionist tradition, which had been in vogue in the 1930s among Swedish family policy experts (see Chapter Two), the report stressed the importance of families as important sites not only for relations between children and parents, and between spouses, but also for maintaining consumption patterns and for facilitating the relationship between individuals (women and men) and the labour market.

The starting point was therefore not so much the functional demands of labour markets, but rather the opposite; how social and economic conditions could and indeed had to be adapted to the functional demands of families. The organisation of household work was one of the main pillars supporting the well-being of families. Homes should be healthy, clean, light, sunny and warm, while clothing should protect from the vagaries of the weather and food should be balanced and nourishing (compare Åkerman, 1945; see also Lövgren, 1993).

Hence, a welfare society was to be built on the basis of families enjoying harmonious social conditions; secure employment and rising material standards were not sufficient. Realising the welfare society necessitated reforms of family practices. The most prominent of the reform initiatives was housing planning. The commission took the notion of the 'healthy home' (*hälsobostaden*) as its starting point. The notion had emerged on the basis of empirical studies of household work, and of the space and design of households. The healthy home was designed to serve both women, working in the household, and men, working outside the confines of the home. The home thus served a dual function as a workplace and a site for relaxation and recovery:

> A spare-time environment should be created within the home, as a counterweight to the monotony and one-sidedness in the daily work for those who are employed outside the household. It is even more important to provide space for creative work for the mothers and the small children, who spend their daily life within the home. (SOU 1947:46, p 30)

Among the tasks contributing to meaningful leisure time, baking, food preservation and handicrafts stood out. The commission also highlighted the need to provide space for children's play, with sufficient room for toys and sleeping places for children.

The commission did not stop at housing conditions, but also saw a need to reform interiors and clothing fashions. It expressed a preference for colourful clothing and interior designs, with modern design inspired by nature and with an individual touch (SOU 1947:46, pp 28-9).

The commission called for the rapid modernisation of housing, with water closets and ergonomic kitchens. Studies had also indicated that much household work was poorly organised and inefficient. Common facilities for cleaning, shopping, maintenance and sewing were proposed as a remedy. More generally, the public provision of services relating to households had to be expanded, including sports facilities, theatres, restaurants, kindergartens and playgrounds.

Consumption was another area deemed ripe for reform, as conventions and advertising led to irrational consumption and wasted money. As a remedy, the commission suggested information and research on the general conditions for consumption (SOU 1947:46, p 25). In modern society, it was argued, consumption norms and patterns were interwoven with family roles and identities. Hence, if economic growth were to be achieved via increasing consumption, families had to be targeted, their different functions understood and the role of the family as consumer reinforced.

The commission inquired into the functional differentiation within modern families and identified women as the nexus of homes and markets in contemporary society. Above all, women took most of the responsibility for housework, functioning as an 'integrating chain within the family and as carers for the children' (SOU 1947:46, p 13). The economic division of labour between spouses was relatively straightforward – they shared the responsibility for the household and for the family income. This was not, the commission claimed, clear from the outset of marriage. To reduce uncertainty over these matters, the commission proposed that copies of the marriage law – with explanatory comments – should be distributed to all newly married couples, and that housing and other common resources should be owned by both spouses, not only the husband. This was to be accompanied by state-provided economic advice to all couples.

The signals sent by the commissions were mixed; indeed, they appeared to operate with a binary understanding of modern families. In their conceptualisation of the home, women had the main responsibility for the household and for the 'inner organisation' of the home, while men were chiefly responsible for the family income. In fact, the whole welfare society was built on the image of the harmonious home, in which the functional nuclear family served as the intermediate link between the state and the market. As such, the nuclear family, with a caring mother and a working father, became a societal unit worth protecting. At the same time, other measures softened the nuclear family contract, for instance by facilitating the sharing of responsibility for family consumption and economic planning, and others still sought to improve relations within families, even at the most intimate level.

Intimate relations

The commissions' interrogations and prescriptions did not stop at the material and social conditions of families. Relations between spouses were also to be reformed, to enhance and improve the connections between women and men within families: 'The formation of a family is built on the attraction between a man and women – erotically and on the basis of a correspondence in temperament, general interests, etc' (SOU 1947:46, p 14).

The commissions of the 1930s and 1940s considered modern relationships to be founded on love and understanding between women and men rather than on economic obligations. Following an increase in social mobility and the relative decline of social and geographical proximity between people, 'the erotic part of marriage selection had become more prominent' (SOU 1947:46, p 14).

Furthermore, marriage was no longer the starting point for sexual relations. As the average age at first marriage for women and men had risen (27 for women, and 29 for men in 1943), sexual experiences preceded marriage in most cases. This was a cause for concern, not primarily because of changes in sexual behaviour as such, but rather because it indicated that the function of marriage, which the commission viewed as the cornerstone of a healthy society, had changed. The institution of marriage had to be more attractive and feasible for younger women and men if it were to be reinforced. This was critically dependent on economic conditions for families, but it was not only material factors that contributed to the attractiveness of marriage.

The commission reported the results of a British study that had highlighted the routine nature of sexual relations within marriage:

> Sexual needs are only poorly satisfied within the ordinary marriage. Sexual life becomes a routine, and a source of physical relaxation rather than a spiritual experience of deeper meaning for the man. For women it is not often even that. The orgasm, the plateau of sexual intercourse for women as well as men, is considered unusual rather than natural. Marital love, even at a sensual level, tends to be dry and uninspired. (SOU 1947:46, p 15)

While this may seem a sombre state of affairs, few of the interviewees in the British study considered their sexual life deficient: 'What secures faithfulness in marriages in general is not so much an intensive sexual satisfaction as a general ethical perspective on marriage and a gradual reduction of erotic needs and an increasing longing for comfort at the expense of romanticism' (SOU 1947:46, p 15).

Assuming a parallel situation in Sweden, the commission feared the continuation of atavistic sexual behaviours. More efficient sex education could counteract outdated attitudes and encourage a more functional sexual life, the commission argued. Another important aspect in the reformation of marriage was the daily interaction between spouses – their habits, temperament and general world view. Again, advice and education (this time of a psychological nature) was expected to alleviate some of the dysfunctions in modern marriages (SOU 1947:46, p 16).

Child rearing was another cause for concern. Contemporary child psychology studies had shown that urban children grew up in insecure environments, in which contact with adults was minimal. Of particular importance for the formation of children's personalities was the contact between mother and child, and the importance of direct contact between children and their parents continued as parents exposed their offspring to different social situations. Given the increasing amount of time children spent outside the home – in school and with friends – the home environment was becoming particularly important, as, the commission argued, it represented security and was the basis for acquiring sound values and role models. Parents faced a daunting task, and the commission admitted that no patent solutions were available (SOU 1947:46, p 21). Turning again to advice and education as possible solutions, the commission advocated investment in research on child psychology to create a foundation for better interventions in family organisation.

As is evident, the commission on home and family had the nuclear family as its model for family organisation. It forcefully articulated the ideal of the male breadwinner and the female household head and made serious inquiries into the organisation of family life. However, its report was never taken up in parliament, unlike the findings of most of the other commissions that have been discussed so far. Some of its proposals surfaced in other commission reports, but it was at odds with the emerging doctrine of labour market policy that emphasised the supply of labour and made its perspectives and suggestions seem quaint and outmoded in the policy discourse of the era. However, it resonated with deep-felt sentiments among both conservatives and social democrats, and its perspectives on the importance of the stable nuclear family for the preservation of society lasted well into the political debates of the 1950s and 1960s. Indeed, the commission presented a clear and undisputable portrayal of the family in the Swedish model.

To sum up, two competing perspectives emerged in family policy debates. On the one hand, women should participate, on equal terms, with men in the labour market, and family policy should be designed to make this possible. On the other hand, the ideal of the housewife thrived, portrayed as a building block for sound families in an era of insecurity and growing demands on families. The trend was clearly in the direction of the former, as evidenced by the commission on childcare.

Childcare: for the best for children and mothers

One of the first commission reports on state childcare was published in 1938 as part of the population commission (SOU 1938: 20). The background to the report was a plea from the association of kindergarten teachers, calling for state support for training and hiring kindergarten teachers (Hatje, 1999).

While this entreaty was well received by the population commission, the resulting proposals were more or less disregarded by the government, possibly because of opposition to the kindergarten teachers' association among leading reformers like Alva Myrdal (Tallberg-Broman, 1995). The issue resurfaced in another report from the population commission that suggested that the state should support and regulate childcare services (SOU 1943:9). This time the proposal went through, and the kindergartens were put under municipal control (Tallberg-Broman, 1995). While very little happened in the matter until the 1960s, a commission report in 1951, in which a group of radical experts outlined a policy to support female employment, functioned as a breaking point and a precursor of things to come. While its proposals were largely neglected at the time, they formed the basis of reform policies in the decades to come.

'The 20th century is the century of children'

When the commission published its 650-page report in 1951, entitled *Day Care and Pre-schools* (SOU 1951:15), it summed up five years' investigation into the need for state childcare and how to meet demand. It has been suggested that the commission's findings reflected clashing opinions on female employment (Hatje, 1999) and the report can indeed be read as a polemic against, for instance, the commission on home and family, which had portrayed household work as the ultimate goal for most, if not all, women. The starting point for this commission was instead how to facilitate the entry of women in the labour market:

> Women's increasing occupational awareness has been a huge and powerful stream through the last few decades, and their demand to participate on an equal social and economic footing in the labour market – not driven by a desire to leave home and children but because society, as some have said, needs their labour, families their salaries, and they themselves the feeling of community in responsibilities and love. Families with both spouses participating in the labour market are becoming more common, which breaks old habits and gives us a hint of a new face of contemporary young families. Even if we all agree that children have a right to their mothers, it is natural that this development forces families into compromises. This highlights the responsibilities of the state to reduce the strains that children experience when their mothers work. (SOU 1951:15, p 10)

Research in child psychology had highlighted the needs of children, needs that could not always be met within the confines of the family: 'Society could no longer withdraw from the responsibility for taking care of pre-school children, which has hitherto been left to individual abilities and imagination' (SOU 1951:15, p 11). The well-being of children was a concern not only for families but also for society as a whole; hence a childcare policy was urgently needed (SOU 1951:15, p 13).

In the 'children's century', the welfare of children was an important concern for parents and the state alike. The public sphere had already shouldered some responsibility, through measures in the health, housing and social policy areas, which had reduced child mortality and overcrowding, and improved the conditions for pregnant and postnatal women. But more had to be done. With rapid social changes, young families had difficulty in adapting to a new social order in which family life and working life were separated. Children existed at the very intersection of these conflicting demands and public institutions had to intervene to lessen the burden on young couples on the verge of forming a family.

Even though the commission must be considered radical in its approach to family organisation and the reach of state intervention, it deliberately and explicitly rejected the radical family policy debate of the 1930s that envisaged a 'new family' in which routine work and the close ties between women and children would dissipate. Such a vision signalled the emergence of a 'thoroughly collectivised society', the commission argued, and it went on to defend current practices: 'On the basis of strong psychological reasons and often with full insight into the caretaking needs of children, a majority of women prefer to stay at home as long as the children are small' (SOU 1951:15, p 54).

While defending existing practices, the commission pointed to some contradictions and difficulties for women and children in need of support. It called for a radical reorientation of obligations and roles within contemporary society:

> The way out of the current dilemmas for women is, however, not to reform the family institution as such or to 'take away' the children from their mothers. What is needed is an open discussion of the hindrances for women to take part in the differentiated activities in society, a discussion that therefore must cover women engaged both in household work and in gainful employment. On the basis of such a discussion of the attitudes and values of women we search for practical reform proposals, for instance concerning collective institutions to support women's work at home and in the labour market. And it is only natural that such a discussion must touch upon the general understanding of what constitutes 'male' and 'female' roles within our homes. (SOU 1951:15, p 53)

This advice, however, was quickly forgotten when it came to practical remedies; here pragmatism once again took over. Women were again the targets of reform, while men disappeared from the policy agenda. Even if the commission did mention the possibility of reforming roles and obligations within the family, it primarily addressed the changing roles of mothers and an accommodation of mother–child interaction. But the commission was clearly very ambivalent, and presented recurrent and alternative perspectives on the issue of family–labour market interaction. Indeed, what it strove for was nothing less than a new contract between a dynamic labour market, family organisation and gender roles:

Even if we all agree on the rights of the child to its mother, we must, now and in the future, make compromises between the need of a mother, the right of families to a better household economy based on female employment, the mother's need for paid employment outside the home, and industry's accelerating demands for female labour. (SOU 1951:15, p 59)

The conclusion drawn was that family policy should be designed to support women to stay at home in the immediate postnatal phase, to be succeeded by the possibility of putting children into day care. This was to be funded and organised by the state, with only limited financial contributions from the families, a service to which every women (and child) would be eligible. The expansion of childcare was motivated not only by the interests of women (and the labour market), but also by the needs of children in contemporary society; the commission, referring again to child psychology studies, found that children were finding it increasingly difficult to work and collaborate in groups. Writing in the aftermath of the Second World War, the commission argued that a primary goal was to foster a democratic spirit among the young; otherwise the democratic ideas tradition was in peril. In state childcare, children would widen their 'sense of community' and 'foster a sense of responsibility for collective ownership' (SOU 1951:15, p 75). Child-care facilities would broaden the horizons of children, and introduce them to other children and to adults other than their parents. It would also compensate for 'deficiencies in the domestic upbringing environment, which may be found in individual cases, for instance when a child has no siblings, or is isolated among its siblings (for instance a boy among several girls)' (SOU 1951:15, p 76). Finally, state childcare was expected to have a positive effect on parents, as they would learn and benefit from the examples of functional day-care centres.

On the basis of this argument, the commission proposed a radical expansion of state childcare facilities. A three-tier system was proposed, with pre-schools for children between the ages of three and seven, day-care institutions for children between six months and three years of age, and comprehensive agricultural day-care centres. Childcare was to be run by the municipalities, but heavily subsidised by the state. In an initial phase, families were to contribute on the basis of income, but in the long run childcare was to be free of charge.

This radical proposal was put on ice, however, and was not taken up again until the 1960s. Until then, childcare remained a marginal public commitment (SOU 1972:27, p 235). The issue returned to the political arena with the family commission's report, which reiterated the analysis and proposals of its predecessor, but again with minimal result (SOU 1955:29). A political issue of greater weight at the time was family counselling, where the state would provide parents with psychological insights to improve family relations and the upbringing of the children. Protecting the nuclear family was at the time a more important family policy agenda than facilitating the entry of women into the labour market.

State family counselling

In the early 1940s, a discussion began on measures to prevent abortion. One of the key instruments in the policy drive was family counselling. The idea first appeared in the report of the commission on abortion (SOU 1944:51) and returned in the 1953 commission on the same topic, which explained increasing numbers of abortions – which had reached 10,000 in 1949 – in terms of the pressures within couples' relationships (SOU 1953:29). Up until then, support for families under strain had been limited to acute psychiatric and obstetric care and preventive measures were non-existent. Hence, with the appointment of yet another commission, the time seemed ripe for more broad-based measures, targeting family relations rather than acute expressions of relationship strain. The new commission therefore proposed the introduction of general family counselling, addressing three family policy dilemmas: declining fertility rates, growing numbers of abortions and an increase in divorce (SOU 1957:33, p 12).

Leaning on research in psychology, psychiatry and sociology, the commission pointed to several factors that could explain these developments. Overarching societal change was, as before, analysed as a consequence of urbanisation and the emergence of industrial society, leading to social destabilisation and rootlessness (as opposed to the assumed stable norms and identities of rural society) (SOU 1957:33, p 28). But modern life did not only present challenges, it was argued – if families could accommodate to the much more varied environment and differentiation of industrial society, this could in fact enrich family life and interaction. But difficulties within families seemed to be on the increase. How could that be explained?

It may be argued that the commission's report paved the way for a new understanding of family relations. It did so by pointing to differences in the situations of women and men and to emotional relations between adults. When, the commission argued, traditional (patriarchal) norms and values collided with a new, more democratic and egalitarian, family structure, ambivalence prevailed. Men lost their traditional unlimited power within the family, while women, having grown used to subservience, felt insecure when they were expected to take on roles beyond those of carer and housewife. When women had begun entering the labour market in larger numbers, they also saw their economic independence grow and with that the opportunity to break out of dysfunctional marriages. Economic independence and labour market connections had also led to a loss of traditional identities, for both women and men, the commission argued.

> Many women with gainful employment have become insecure about their tasks and carry conscious or unconscious feelings of guilt for neglecting one thing or another. For a married woman without gainful employment, the current situation may lead to worries. She compares herself to her employed peers and believes that they lead a more satisfying and harmonious life than she does. Pressure also comes for

the married man. He too becomes insecure and jarred by a feeling of lacking freedom at home. He becomes uncertain about the ambitions of his wife and begins to compare his marriage with imagined and often idealised marriages with other women. (SOU 1957:33, p 30)

Adding to this uncertainty was the 'constant talk about divorce', which, it was argued, suggested that this was the only way to resolve conflicts (SOU 1957:33, p 30). The divorce discourse was the primary target for intervention, the commission argued. Preventive talks with professional family counsellors could solve what were often imagined and overly exaggerated difficulties by helping couples gain 'emotional maturity' (SOU 1957:33, p 30). In doing so, welfare policies would not only provide material support, thus stabilising the economic conditions for women and men, but also emotional support and guidance to reduce the pressures of modern society.

The analysis was firmly anchored in contemporary sociological theory, in particular the works of the Swedish sociologist Torgny Segerstedt on man's conditions in industrial society (Segerstedt and Lundquist, 1949). According to Segerstedt's writings, technical advances brought with them more complex social identities. Women and men were forced to become more reflective in relation to all the factors that were shaping their living conditions. At the same time, the family remained a core group in society, and increasingly so, as the anomic factors called for secure spaces to hide from the contingencies of industrial society. Segerstedt also subscribed to a Durkheimian understanding of the virtues of functional differentiation: the more specialised work had become, the more dependent people were becoming on one another. Hence, the stronger the demarcations between gainful and household employment, the stronger the interdependence between the two and the stronger the unity of the family. However, the so-called functional nature of families was in need of adaptation. The relationship between the spouses had to be enforced through family counselling. Counselling was also needed to reduce the pressures of family life that led to abortion and divorce (SOU 1957:33, p 124 onwards). In sharp contrast to its counterparts in the 1930s and early 1940s, the commission strongly objected to genetic counselling, deeming it 'a very complex area' (SOU 1957:33, p 103).

In Bill no. 135, the government outlined its view of family counselling, paying homage to earlier debates on the issue, especially the issues of abortion prevention and the organisation of family life, observing the broad backing for proposals to link abortion prevention to family counselling. While noting that family counselling had primarily served to aid families in acute distress – through psychiatric care, and maternity and paediatric care – it pointed out the need to widen its remit, and in doing so broaden its knowledge base to the fields of psychology and sociology (Bill 1960, no. 135, p 13). While acknowledging the family counselling initiatives that were already in place – run by municipalities, hospitals and churches – the government also criticised the existing system for being fragmented and disparate

– 'in fact, the institutions have little else in common than the name – family counselling agency' (Bill 1960, no. 135, p 14).

On the basis of these considerations, the government proposed to introduce a system of general family counselling – including abortion advice and social and medical support for women and men – funded and regulated by the state. The proposal sailed easily through parliament.

Implementing universal maternity insurance

While there had been general consensus on most of the welfare reforms hitherto, the political discussion surrounding the issue of maternity insurance remained. The reforms enacted in the 1940s were seen as piecemeal and in need of a major overhaul. The most important issue to resolve was whether the insurance was to be universal or based on the principle of income replacement. This issue was relegated to the commission on social insurance. The debate on the maternity insurance, together with that on child allowance, became a defining moment in Swedish social policy. Its remit was to investigate the preconditions for a mandatory income-related sickness insurance that also incorporated industrial injury insurance (Lindqvist, 1989). In contrast to many of the other commissions of the time, this one worked tightly integrated with the Ministry for Social Affairs, signalling the political importance of the issue and of the policy principles to be established (Lindqvist, 1989).

Much was at stake; not only was a previously fragmented and occupation-based insurance to be centralised and put under state control, but also the principle of income replacement was to be established. Hence, the proposal was an integral part of an ideological reorientation within the Social Democratic Party, in the direction of the homogenisation and coordination of a hitherto very disparate set of instruments (Lindqvist, 1989, p 68).

The social insurance commission also covered the varied instruments for support for pregnant and postnatal women (SOU 1954:4). Its proposal was to introduce general maternity insurance as part of the general sickness insurance. The insurance would be next to universal, the only remaining exceptions being incapacitated women. A two-tier system was proposed, in which all women would be guaranteed support for delivery costs and a basic maternity allowance. A second tier would be based on the income replacement principle. The funding was similar to the sickness insurance, based on a combination of state support and payroll taxes (SOU 1954:4, p 84). Means-tested motherhood support was to remain in place, functioning as a safety net for the poorest mothers (SOU 1954:4, p 81).

The proposal to coordinate maternity support was subject to heated debate in parliament. Two different types of critique emerged in the debate: from the right, and from within social democracy. Conservatives and liberals (with some support from the Agrarian Party) argued that the background reports were insufficient and that they had systematically neglected the housewives' perspective. As a remedy, they proposed a voluntary second-tier insurance, as well as the inclusion of housewives within the motherhood aid programme. A few social democrats opposed the two-tier system, advocating instead a universal system on a higher level than the existing universal measure, motherhood aid. Somewhat paradoxically, this proposal resonated with the conservatives (motion no. 492, FK, and no. 633, AK, 1954; motion no. 468, FK, and no. 601, AK, 1954). Added to this, some experts on the commission had voiced reservations against the proposal as such, primarily for reasons of state finance.

Other social policy measures had met with mixed responses from the bourgeois parties, some critical and some more positive. However, when it came to this proposal, the conservatives, liberals and agrarians joined in their critique of the government Bill; not only did the proposal neglect the welfare of housewives, it also contributed to a centralisation (and socialisation) of the welfare system by integrating all existing schemes in a state-organised system. The first line of criticism focused on housewives, as the parties feared a deterioration of their social standing if the government Bill became law:

> That working mothers are compensated for loss of income is only natural to me, and it is a natural consequence of security legislation in the area. It cannot be helped, however, that the support strongly underrates the work that women employed in the household do.... The woman who works in the household must not be given or kept in the perception that society does not appreciate her efforts or does not value her work. (Conservative MP Hagård, AK protocol no. 19, 1954, p 71)

What was at stake was nothing less than the social status of the housewife, and the bourgeois parties were clearly suspicious of the intentions of the government. Similarly, they surmised the motives for the organisation of the maternity insurance, detecting a return of the socialist inclinations of the government. The social democrats responded that their proposal resolved a major social policy dilemma, namely the inclusion of all women. In the words of Nancy Eriksson, a prominent female member of parliament:

> We have a solution that not only compensates for the wage loss of women employed in industry but also a general insurance that covers all mothers. The insurance issue has not been resolved category by category, but for all women who give birth. (AK protocol no. 19, 1954, p 76)

On a similar note, Minister for Social Affairs Gunnar Sträng defended the mandatory, state second-tier insurance, arguing that a voluntary system would become overly complicated, bureaucratic and unequal. Furthermore, the inclusion of women employed in the household would create inequalities, as, Sträng argued, housewives were not subject to the same pressures experienced through gainful employment (AK protocol no. 19, 1954, p 81).

By the end of the day, the government proposal met with only limited resistance in both chambers of parliament; the only difference was that the Second Chamber – after a motion from the Conservative Party – wanted all women to be covered, not just those in gainful employment. This was, however, overruled in the First Chamber, where the social democrats had a stable majority. Hence, broad coverage and inclusion in a state-funded and publicly organised system had been established as principles not only for the sickness insurance but also for maternity support. What remained a controversial issue was motherhood aid. It was the subject of the first report of the social policy commission (SOU 1961:38), a commission consisting only of the top echelon of the labour market parties. In this report, which proposed that motherhood aid should be abolished (which later became the government's proposal and the decision taken in parliament), motherhood insurance was solely discussed in the context of labour market relations and gainful employment. With this report, the last remaining elements of the housewife discourse seemed to have vanished. The commission report echoed the government's stance in the 1957 debates, viewing the social insurance system as an integrated whole, together with sickness insurance, and the basic and second-tier pension systems (SOU 1961:38, p 56 onwards).

Conclusion

Gender, work and the welfare state

The economic governance model that was outlined by the end of the 1940s set the ambitious goals of full employment, high growth, low inflation and improved social conditions. To make these seemingly incompatible goals feasible, a broad array of economic policy measures were established with an active labour market policy at the centre (collectively known as the Rehn–Meidner model). The full employment pledge, however, applied only to the male labour force, whereas women still functioned as a labour market reserve. Women in the labour market also worked under different conditions with lower salaries.

The economic policy model emerged in conjunction with a massive expansion of social welfare, comprising, inter alia, public unemployment support and universal child allowances, sickness benefits and basic pensions. The growth of universal welfare commitments, together with the Rehn–Meidner model, constituted the Swedish model. An important part of the Swedish model was a further expansion of family policies, thereby reforming the everyday life of nuclear families.

The debate on women's paid and unpaid work continued during the 1940s. The debate on the family paradox, which had been established in the 1930s, intensified; how could the housewife ideal be sustained when powerful actors in the labour market wanted to improve the opportunities for women to procure gainful employment (which in itself was motivated less by gender equality per se than by the desire to reduce tensions on the labour market)? The complicated relationship between paid and unpaid work therefore came into the forefront of family policy debates, and was intertwined with the provision of care.

Gender, care and the welfare state

Contemporary understandings of care were embedded in the deepening paradoxical relationship between paid and unpaid work. Some argued for a social policy supporting family relations and enabling women to stay at home. In such discourses, married women emerged as responsible for the well-being of families and for practical duties in the home, serving as a uniting emotional link within the family and a provider of care. The division of labour within families was explained and defended by nuclear family apologists portraying women as 'caring heads' and men as income providers.

There was discord in the debate, however, and opposing voices, such as that of Alva Myrdal, called for more ambitious labour market and social policies, including an expansion of state childcare. They outlined a new role for the state and family policy, resolving the paradox and supporting women in their combined roles in working life and in the family. They leaned on an understanding of contemporary (industrial) society characterised by functional differentiation with individuals becoming increasingly interdependent. Moreover, proponents of this perspective argued that it was necessary for women to have gainful employment for many reasons. First of all, it was positively related to women's well-being, but it was also seen as necessary to enhance the supply of labour and pre-empt expected labour shortages. Subsequently, a discussion of the preconditions for gender equality began, for instance on 'women's two roles'.

These perspectives developed in parallel, but the latter came to dominate the social and family policy debate as the demand for female labour grew and resulted in the marginalisation of the housewife ideal. Nevertheless, the conceptual framing of the family in the Swedish model was anchored in the stable nuclear family where the mother was constructed as the caring consumer and the father as the breadwinner. Hence, women were still the targets of family policy reforms. However, it can be argued that new family policy paradoxes emerged with the attempts to reconcile the contradictory family ideals.

(Gender) equality in the post-war period

Family policy revolved around women and their roles in the family and, to some extent, in the labour market, and the interplay between the domestic demands and the dynamics of the post-war labour market, where the search for new sources of labour power accelerated. No drastic change from the 1930s could be discerned; equality debates revolved around class relations, where gender equality was relegated to a residual role. Gender equality in itself was still equated with women's equality. However, there were signs of a shift, primarily as labour market conditions seemed to call for reforms facilitating women's entry into the labour market. Radical voices even called for a debate on women and men's roles in the family and within society in the wake of the imbalances in the labour market.

Towards the end of the 1950s, the debate was further radicalised when emotionally poor marriages emerged as a new reform area. This reform line emerged – and not for the first in time in Swedish history – in a government commission system where a study of men and women and their relationships had recently been presented. This paved the way for a new understanding of gender relations beyond the notions of functional differentiation and interdependence. If women and men were unsatisfied in modern marriages because of the consequences of industrialisation – witnessed in increasing numbers of abortions and divorces – gender equality was perhaps the only remedy at disposal. Hence, gender equality emerged as a political panacea to two political challenges, labour market stability and social reproduction.

Consequently, gender equality within marriage became a political project. Gender equality beyond marriage was still waiting to be articulated as a policy ambition.

Notes

[1] The Rehn-Meidner model was named by the LO (Swedish Trade Union Confederation) economists Gösta Rehn and Rudolf Meidner.

[2] Negotiations between the government, the LO and the employers were held in order to create stability in the labour market, marked by intense conflicts and high unemployment. The government (the Social Democratic Party) threatened legislation if the parties failed to arrive at long-term agreements. The two main organisations, LO and SAF (the Swedish Employers' Federation), however, decided in 1936 that they would try to avoid involving the state, which finally resulted in the signing of the Saltsjöbaden Agreement, or the Main Agreement of 1938 (Edlund, 1989). The agreement meant that LO achieved the same status as the employers, resulting in two equal parties. At the same time, pay talks for all the unions in LO were centralised and coordinated, and a framework agreement was reached. The Saltsjöbaden Agreement, together with the centralised wage negotiation, put an end to the strained relations that the labour market had suffered for several decades (Edlund, 1989). The Saltsjöbaden Agreement was historic. It is described in the literature as an accord or a compromise between labour and capital (Korpi, 1979; Rothstein, 1986; Therborn, 1989; Misgeld et al, 1992). The Saltsjöbaden Agreement was thus an important starting point for the creation of the Swedish model.

[3] This was not an exclusively conservative standpoint; up until the mid-1940s, it was embraced by some social democrats, including the Myrdals (Therborn, 1989, p 21 onwards).

FOUR

Towards gender-neutral ideals and gender equality politics

> We should stop hammering in the concept of 'women's two roles'. Both men and women have *one* lead role, that as human beings. The role as human beings entails, as a necessity and as a moral obligation, but also a sweet experience and much else, taking care of your offspring. If one does not admit that, one should understand that one contributes to making women's liberation what it is now: a paroled liberation. Woman has only been set free under the implicit condition that she sees her main task to be to care for and foster her children and create an environment in which to bring them up. (Moberg, 2003 [1961], p 14)

Eva Moberg, author and debater, wrote these words in the edited volume *Young Liberals*. Her article came to play a large role in a debate that resulted in the transformation of family policy in the 1960s. The issues that she raised – whether caring were a task only for women, and whether women were only 'on probation' – disturbed the equilibrium of the family debate, which, despite all the reforms that had been enacted in the 1940s and 1950s, still glorified motherhood and the nuclear family.

Eva Moberg was not alone in showcasing the lack of gender equality. The new women's movement grew strong in the 1960s, demanding changes both in the political system and within the family. At the same time, family experts, from Norway and Sweden, from within psychology, sociology and education, studied the social processes behind gender differences and inequality between women and men. By highlighting how 'sex roles' were socially constructed, they claimed that they could explain how women became subordinated in society (Dahlström et al, 1962).

With a different starting point from the women's movement, but with similar aims, came the labour market parties. Their primary concern was to reduce the labour shortages of the period, which seemed to necessitate a much more structured inflow of women into the labour market. This, in turn, was an integral part of the active labour market policy, and the policy hegemon of the era, the National Labour Market Board (AMS).

As a result of the vivid and radical years of the 1960s, family policy reforms changed direction in the 1970s, from a focus on families and family functions, where women were the primary target for family policy reforms, to gender-neutral ideals and gender equality in a wider context, in particular equality in the labour market. An early example was the reformed taxation system, which introduced individual taxation (the reform came two years before the gender-neutral parental insurance reform in 1973). Equal treatment in the public sector was legally mandated in 1976, and a year later the labour market parties reached an agreement on equality for the private sector. In 1979, parents with children under the age of eight were given the legal right to work six hours per day, and in the same year a gender equality Act was established (Hirdman, 1990). The 1970s were indeed marked by intense efforts to establish gender equality in the home and in the labour market. These efforts, however, came to be criticised, mainly because of an in-built paradox: gender neutrality turned out to exist only on a legislative level and not in social practice in working life or in the home where gender discrimination remained a huge problem and unequal gender relations prevailed. It was mainly feminist researchers who highlighted the paradox at the beginning of the 1980s. However, during the period analysed in this chapter, gender neutrality was seen as a means to achieve gender equality – in the workplace as well as in the home.

Thus, the family policy paradox of work–family balance disappeared in policy discourse. It was assumed to have been solved by targeting fathers in gender-neutral reforms. It can therefore be argued that during times of great policy change, former conflicts disappear but only for a limited time and only in order to appear again in another shape and form. The 1960s and 1970s was indeed a time of great policy change, and the family paradoxes that have been discussed in previous chapters disappeared in policy debate and discourse. However, yet another paradox was emerging, a development that will be discussed in Chapter Five.

This chapter highlights some factors that led to the overhauling of family policy (Dahlström et al, 1962; Hirdman, 1990, 1998; Acker et al, 1992; Florin and Karlsson, 2000; Klinth, 2002). Some of them will be dealt with more extensively than others,[1] but first, the work of the family policy committees of the 1960s is scrutinised. The chapter goes on to analyse the path towards the 1970 tax reform, when joint taxation was abolished, and the background of the highly influential equality report to the 1969 Social Democratic Party congress. These events culminated in the introduction of gender-neutral family policy reforms in the beginning of the 1970s. The chapter analyses one of these in particular, namely the gender-neutral parental insurance reform. It was not only mothers and fathers who were analysed in the parental insurance reform; the 'best interests of children' were also covered. Thus, this section examines the emerging debate on children's place and situation in the Swedish welfare state, and how they could fit into the gender-equal family. The chapter ends with an introduction of the gender equality Act that was passed in 1979.

Family policy debates in the early 1960s

Despite the many family policy reforms already undertaken, the urge to widen the debate remained strong. Some initiatives were more wide-ranging and ambitious than others. Two male social democratic members of parliament went as far as to propose a general review of the entire policy field (motion no. 140, FK, 1960). The motive for their proposal was the continuing difficulties that young families faced, which, according to the MPs, showed that the reforms carried out so far had been insufficient. With fertility rates declining, they predicted a return to the population crisis of the 1930s. Under these circumstances, there was an urgent need to investigate further the dynamics of the population issue: 'What surprises ... those who wish to approach and penetrate this problem is the limited number of scientific studies of the factors that determine population dynamics. Not least welcome in the current situation would be sociological evaluations of the ideas and group attitude that contribute to shaping this area' (motion no. 140, FK, 1960).

Among the factors that acted as a constraint to starting a family, material factors stood out, not least the shortage of housing. Legal and social factors also played a part. Changes in labour market regulation had not prevented discrimination against women with children. Given the lack of childcare, families were faced with the difficult choice between children or a higher income, a dilemma that, the social democratic MPs argued, called for a renewed interest in the relationship between motherhood and employment. The motion was discarded in parliament, but it is nevertheless relevant for our purposes as it captures the spirit of the 1960s, when the family policy debate again became radicalised after the relatively complacent period of the 1940s and 1950s. While the first attempt was defeated, the reformers were more successful in 1962, when the chairperson of the Social Democratic Woman's Association, Nancy Eriksson, together with other female social democratic MPs, presented a motion along similar lines (motion no. 584, AK, 1962, similar to motion no. 511, FK, 1962).

While content with the reforms already pursued, Eriksson and her collaborators pointed out the need to reduce the pressures on families with children, and on single mothers. As a starting point, they proposed that a government commission on the cost of children should be set up. Family policy reforms, they argued, had hitherto been designed under other circumstances than the existing ones, and new reforms had to take into account, for example, that unemployment was non-existent and that incomes, and expectations in general, were on the increase. The main problem to be resolved concerned the imbalance between rising economic wealth and declining fertility levels. This, Eriksson and her colleagues argued, could only reflect the economic insecurity of families with children, and in particular the negative economic impact of having children; if women stayed at home, families would lose one of their incomes, but if women went out to work, families would be burdened by the costs (and other limitations) of existing childcare, scarce and ill-equipped as it was at the time.

Eriksson and her colleagues gained support from other members and parliament decided in favour of the proposition for a new population commission, and so, in 1962 yet another family policy commission was appointed (Familjeberedningen), staffed with academics and top-level state officials and given a mandate to analyse shortcomings in public services for families with children.

Family policy as social justice and freedom of choice

Already within the first year of the commission's existence, family policy ambitions were mounting. Responding to a growing number of women in the labour market, the government proposed to increase the number of day-care places. The reason for this was that labour market participation among women with children under the age of seven had increased from 31% to 36.7% in just two years, between 1961 and 1963. This had not been met with adequate family policy measures, the government admitted. For instance, only 450 new day-care places had been created between 1954 and 1963 (Bill 1963, no. 62, pp 3 and 5). This situation would now change; in the 1963 Bill, the government pressed for a substantial amount of funding for an increase in the number of day-care centres. The proposal was accepted without any further debate in parliament. The public sector grew very fast in the following years, with enormous consequences for women and children especially. We return to this subject later in the chapter.

While the family policy debate in the parliament and within the commission system often concerned policy details, it also touched on the frames and discourses in which family policy was couched. The hegemonic population policy discourse was increasingly questioned, primarily by liberals and social democrats, who suggested that family policy should be framed only in terms of social justice and freedom of choice for the individual. Social justice and freedom of choice pertained in particular to women – men were notably still excluded from the discourse. An expansion of public childcare, it was argued in a commission report from 1964, offered women a new liberty, that of not having to choose between children and employment.

> Making the freedom of choice complete entails families having the economic security to have as many children as they choose to, even if some families becomes larger than then' normal family'. It also means relieving woman from the choice between children and work; rather it enables her to do both as a woman and as an individual. (SOU 1964:36, p 32)

In the debate, reforms were now focusing on individuals, especially women and children, instead of emphasising population policy arguments in relation to family policy reforms and debates. Men were still excluded from the analysis, although this was to change in the coming years.

The emergence of the gender-equal family

When social justice and freedom of choice entered the political vocabulary, the gender-equal family became the new political catchphrase. Equality and female employment became salient features in reforms of the social insurance system, backed not least by the labour market parties (Klinth, 2002, p 110).

The labour market parties acted on the basis of a conviction that the connection between increasing female labour market participation and reforms in social insurance were crucial and this view became the focal point for the Committee on Family Policy established in 1965. The committee did not, however, act in solitude; for example, in 1966, the Swedish Trade Union Confederation (LO) congress took the decision in principle to urge the introduction of a gender-neutral insurance system, in effect confronting the male-breadwinner model with a new ideal, that of the dual-breadwinner family (Klinth, 2002, p 113).

Another challenge to the post-war family compact came from the debate on the tax system. This had been going on for some time, but intensified in the late 1960s when taxes were integrated into the family policy and gender debates (SOU 1967:52). Indeed, when the 'biggest tax reform of the century' was conceived, the family policy impact of the tax system was an integral, and dominant, motive. But the route to a gender-neutral tax system was not straightforward.

Towards individual taxation

One of the key decisions shaping current Swedish family policy was the tax reform of the 1970s, when joint (family) taxation was abolished and replaced with individual taxation. This marked the end of a debate that had been going on for more than 70 years and had intensified after the war. The issue had been the subject of several government commissions. One, from 1959, had a primarily technical approach, and deemed it difficult to change the existing system. Instead, the commission proposed an intensified public campaign on joint taxation (SOU 1959:13, p 47 onwards).

The 1964 tax commission remained steadfast in its support of joint taxation (Elvander, 1972). Despite this, the Minister of Finance Gunnar Sträng argued in the 1965 finance plan that the issue was in need of further investigation, as joint taxation had not only some technical limitations but also a detrimental effect on economic equality. Sträng was, however, reluctant to make a switch without a more penetrating investigation, fearing that only some groups would benefit from separate taxation. Hence, a new commission, the family taxation commission, was appointed in 1965. To complicate matters somewhat, one of the mandates of the family taxation commission was to shed light on the subject of joint taxation. In one of its reports, the commission questioned the dominant notion that families formed an organic entity of husbands and wives, where the ability to pay taxes was determined not individually but jointly (SOU 1967:52):

> Joint taxation may be seen as leading to imbalances between families with and without children, as well as between families where both spouses have gainful employment and those in which only one of the spouses has an income while the other is working in the household. Recently, labour market policy aspects have been raised against joint taxation. The joint taxation of spouses has been said to impact

negatively on married women's propensity to take part in the labour market. Such an effect of taxation would be unfortunate with the shortages in the labour market and at a time when married women constitute the only major labour reserve of importance. (SOU 1967:52, p 52)

The commission made a thorough investigation of state support for families, and single parents, with children, arguing that all should be covered by a single, but differentiated system of consumption support, composed of child allowance and income-related family support. The commission therefore viewed economic support for families and the taxation system as unified and mutually dependent, even though it stressed that a new system had to compensate for the loss of certain aspects of the joint taxation system, such as the tax deduction for married women with children and for single mothers.

Hence, the ambition to create a system of individual taxation intervened in a string of controversial political issues, including responsibility for childcare, economic redistribution, labour market relations and the supply of labour, all of which were to be blended in a new taxation system.

Nevertheless, in 1969, the family taxation commission presented its final report and suggested individual taxation. After the commission's suggestions had been submitted for consideration by all relevant bodies, the Minister of Finance Gunnar Sträng was able to go ahead with the proposal on individual taxation (Elvander, 1972).

The 1970 Bill proposed two major changes in the taxation system: first, the introduction of individual taxation, and second, a reduction in the taxation of income for a large part of the population. Individual taxation was implemented in 1971. The political scientist Nils Elvander argued that the Bill was a compromise, an attempt to overcome the complicated opposition between a fairer distribution of income among different groups and dimensions regarding equality (Elvander, 1972, p 287).

Public debates in the wake of the taxation question

The transition from family to individual taxation was preceded by intense and sometimes very harsh debates. One of the driving forces behind reform was the 'sex-role debate' of the 1960s, which, in conjunction with the push from the labour market parties, created an irresistible political force for the modernisation of the tax system (Elvander, 1972, p 252).

However, this is very much a retrospective construction; in reality, the road to the individualisation of taxation was protracted and anything but predetermined. The starting point was modest: a critique of existing 'sex roles' and prejudices against women in the labour market, articulated by social scientists and newspaper columnists in the early 1960s. Taxation was seen as the key to changes in both respects; joint taxation discriminated against families with children, and put a premium on the sole provider of incomes, whereas a second income was actually a burden on the family organisation (given the scarce supply of childcare). Hence, the taxation system cemented sex roles and the subordination of women, and the imprisonment of women as household workers (Elvander, 1972, p 257).

This position found some resonance with the Social Democratic Party, and with the trade union federations for blue- and white-collar workers (LO and Central Organisation of Salaried Employees [TCO], respectively), even though their support was conditional and somewhat tepid. Outright critique of an individualised taxation system came from some of the trade unions – notably the Swedish Confederation of Professional Associations (SACO) but also the LO – and from the Social Democratic Women's Association. What this broad and complex group of critiques shared was a defence of the family as an economic unit. Thus, taxation reform cut across the political and organisational spectrum, leading to some unexpected interest coalitions and to divisions within the trade unions and the political parties (Florin, 1999, p 112 onwards).

Perhaps the greatest divide occurred within the Social Democratic Women's Association. Many of its prominent representatives were housewives, including its chairperson Nancy Eriksson, who argued that women's liberation did not necessarily depend on women's gainful employment. Others, including veterans like Alva Myrdal, and Karin Kock, an economist, sided with the reformers, viewing individual taxation as a liberating force for working–class women. In the midst of the taxation debates, the Social Democratic Women's Association elected a new chairperson, Lisa Mattson, who pledged to make the organisation more 'women-friendly' and 'professional' for working women. This paved the way for a reorientation among female social democrats (Florin, 1999, p 116).

Engaging the entire political spectrum, taxation also became an issue for public mobilisation, epitomised by the Family Campaign. This was organised to combat the political currents of individual taxation and the sex-role debate, in defence of the housewife ideal. Influenced by the radicalisation of political expressions at the time (but perhaps not the content of that radicalisation), the campaign went as far as threatening to occupy the Ministry of Finance to support its case (Florin, 1999, p 126 onwards).

As we have seen, many actors were engaged in the debate on individual taxation. The question became a symbol of the major changes that the 1960s debate on family and gender relations came to reveal. By the end of the 1960s, the question of equality was one of the most important issues for the government. This became obvious in the 1969 congress of the Social Democratic Party.

Social democracy and gender equality

An important step towards a gender-neutral family policy discourse was taken at the 1969 congress of the Social Democratic Party (SAP). The congress showcase was a report on equality, written by a group of LO and SAP representatives to outline the activities to reduce inequality in Sweden and throughout the world.

Equality was therefore very broadly defined, and the party congress enumerated a long list of areas to be covered under the banner of equality.

It included, among other things, equal living conditions and equal access to power and influence in society, including economic and industrial democracy. Equality was seen as an overriding societal concern, relevant to all, not only to the poor and dispossessed. It should mark policies in practices in schools, workplaces, organisations and homes, held together under a new political umbrella, equality politics (Jämlikhet, 1969, p 16).

This would cover virtually all policy fields, from the labour market, housing and education to justice and taxation, working together towards the ultimate goal of a classless society (compare this with the debate on gender mainstreaming during the 1990s discussed in Chapter Five).

It was clear that this was something other than the rather bland policy discourse of the 1950s and early 1960s. Alva Myrdal, who presented the report to the congress, blended biblical connotations – 'equal before God' – with slogans of the French Revolution (*'liberté, égalité, fraternité'*) and the classic liberal dictum of 'equal life chances for all'. But social democracy had higher ambitions than that:

> All have the right to a share of the total resources in society. This demand, and also the demand for economic democracy, is the significant and determining demand of equality for social democracy.... We have succeeded earlier in realising the equality demands of the era. And so we shall, with the vital force residing in our popular movement, realise a policy which will reshape our society into one in which equality approaches the ideal of classlessness. (*Jämlikhet*, 1969, pp 164-5)

Family policy was given special attention in the programme, and three areas were singled out as particularly important for achieving equality: substantial equality between men and women; eradication of inequalities between different cohabitation forms; and a levelling out of living conditions between families of different size (*Jämlikhet*, 1969, p 93). With the advent of an equal society, women, men and children would be released from stereotyped roles and positions:

> From all viewpoints, increasing equality would lead to considerable advantages. Men would become more active in the values of family life, for instance through better contacts with their children. Women would become more economically independent, and from having work colleagues and contacts with environments outside the home. The greatest gain of increasing equality would of course be that no one was forced into a predetermined role based on their sex, but instead have greater opportunities to develop their own personal traits. Children's development would also be positively affected by more contacts with both sexes. Equality also gives preconditions for greater economic security through the twin incomes. (*Jämlikhet*, 1969, p 94)

The route towards increasing equality was primarily one of individualisation. The individual was to be the subject of reform, and not, as had been the case before, the family. Individuals should be treated equally, irrespective of whether they were living alone or in some form of cohabitation. Family law therefore had to be reformed in relation to inheritance, marriage, marriage rights and so on, as did labour market policy and taxation. All ensuing laws should reinforce the economic independence of the individual as the cornerstone of equality.

Children were included in the equality discourse. Inequalities between adopted and non-adopted children should be abolished, the report argued. Furthermore, not only married couples but also unmarried partners should be eligible for adoption. The report also urged for reforms in inheritance law to support children with special needs relating to their age or educational development.

Despite the recurrent, almost ubiquitous, talk of individualisation, the report still cherished the idea of the nuclear family. However, it was a reformed nuclear family that the report anticipated – the dual-breadwinner nuclear family. To reach this goal, the report urged reforms in areas such as unemployment insurance and the legal regulation of leave in connection with childbirth. For example, housewife insurance was to be made gender-neutral, so as to enable 'house husbands' to work at home. The most significant proposal was to make the maternity insurance gender-neutral, thereby enabling men to take parental leave. Altogether, the ambition was to recreate the welfare system and to give it a new, broader mission, or, in the words of Alva Myrdal: 'When we attempt to put equality politics into a broader perspective, we realise how systematically coherent it must be. Then we understand how much it demands of radical reconsiderations and of political will' (*Jämlikhet*, 1969, p 174).

The 1969 Social Democratic Party congress made the report a guide to the future work of the party board and the parliamentary group. This was not mere lip service; the series of family proposals that came in the 1970s were rooted in the discussions that had been pursued in the 1960s, many of which ended up in the equality report and the congress debates. The most prominent were the aforementioned taxation reforms, and the transformation of the maternity insurance into a gender-neutral parental insurance.

However, while family policy was being transformed and gender-neutral ideals introduced, the Swedish economy was going through a deep crisis. The tension between reform ambitions and economic instability are explored later.

The Swedish model reconsidered, 1970-79

The oil crisis of 1973 shook the preconditions for economic policy making and for the ever-expending reform agenda of Swedish social policy. The first signs of a breakdown of the structured coherence between regulation and economic growth patterns, however, began to show as early as the mid-1960s. With the oil crisis and the ensuing sharp decline in economic activity, institutional arrangements became increasingly pressured (Jessop, 2002). Centralised bargaining was marked by increasing friction and the bargaining rounds were affected by internal tensions among both employers and unions. The hegemony of the export sector in wage determination was questioned when public sector employment expanded (employees in the public sector were organised by the LO) (Kjellberg, 1992; Benner, 1997; Åmark, 1998; Nycander, 2002).

Despite the economic fluctuations, the flow of social policy reforms had not come to an end. On the contrary, in the general parliamentary debate in January 1973, Prime Minister Olof Palme presented the social policy targets: unemployment insurance would be improved, dental insurance introduced, sickness insurance made more generous (and relabelled 'sickness pay'), supplementary pensions increased, support for the disabled enhanced and housing support for low-income groups without children established. More was to come; the basic pension system, public support for day care, sickness pay for parents who stay at home with sick children, and a gender-neutral parental insurance were also on the list of planned reforms. More broadly, the social democratic government pledged to secure full employment while protecting the environment and widening democratic participation (parliamentary protocol, Allmänpolitisk debatt [debate on general political issues], 31 January 1973).

It must be said that the reforms were, in fact, presented before the economic downturn; what is noteworthy is that little changed with the crisis. Indeed, the general perception, not only of the government but also of influential economists, was that the crisis was cyclical and that there would be a return growth pattern in due course, given that public authorities supported companies and employment during the downturn (Lundqvist, 2001).

Some large-scale public industrial projects were also devised, including a major steel mill in Luleå in northern Sweden and the expansion of the Kockums shipyard in Malmö in the south, and several nuclear power plants around the country (Schön, 2000). As late as 1975, the social democratic government claimed that it had pursued economic policies that stabilised domestic demand and domestic industrial production, thereby dampening the negative impact of international economic volatility. However, beginning in late 1975, the volatility of the preceding years was succeeded by an unequivocal depression, with shrinking markets, a rapid economic slowdown and negative economic growth. Massive rationalisations ensued, hitting energy-intensive industries in particular, such as iron ore, paper and pulp (Schön, 2000, p 489 onwards). Public industrialisation projects, with the notable exception of nuclear energy, were halted or scrapped altogether. The shipbuilding industry, once the industrial pride of Sweden (as the world's second-largest producer) nearly vanished altogether and other sectors, such as textiles, steel and forestry, crumbled under the pressure.

In 1976, after 44 years in office, the Social Democratic Party lost the election, and the chairman of the Centre Party (formerly the Agrarian Party), Thorbjörn Fälldin, became prime minister, forming a government with the Liberal Party (Folkpartiet) and Conservative Party (Moderata samlingspartiet). The new government was instantly thrown into crisis management mode; just a few days after it had taken office, industrial firms began to ask for state support (Åsling, 1979). After futile attempts to entice firms to cope with the downturn themselves, the state intervened in sector after sector of the economy, providing credits and loans and in some cases even nationalising industries (Benner, 1997).

In the midst of the economic crisis, relations in the labour market turned sour, culminating in the largest dispute in the Swedish labour market in 70 years, the 'Big Conflict' of 1980. This was the outcome of a revolt by the public sector unions against the hegemonic role of the export sectors as wage leaders in wage bargaining. This highlighted the classic divisive issue between the public and the export sector – the question of whether the production of goods was really so much more valuable (and therefore better paid) than the production of care. The conflict marked the end of the hegemony of the large, internationalised firms and the export industry unions within industrial relations (Kjellberg, 1992).

Despite the economic and institutional crises, there was, as argued earlier, no paucity of social reforms. The retirement age was lowered to 65, there was an increase in state subsidies for medication and hospital treatment, as well as in compensation levels in unemployment insurance (Marklund, S. 1988). The expansion of public service provision, and in particular childcare and care for the elderly, continued, and between the late 1960s and the beginning of 1980s, 500,000 women entered the labour market, many of whom joined the public sector (Axelsson, 1991). In order to enable women to work, public day care continued to expand, and, with this came what was perhaps one of the most important reforms of the time – the introduction of gender-neutral parental insurance, discussed next.

Parental insurance

Maternity insurance had been discussed extensively during the latter part of the 1960s, initially shaped by persistent political divisions concerning women's work. When the commission finalised its work, consensus had superseded conflict and all political parties, from left to right, backed the idea of a gender-neutral parental insurance (Klinth, 2002, p 182 onwards). The Family Policy Committee, established in 1965, was the main vehicle for the proposal. Its final report was a powerful representation of the new policy discourse and policy practice. The change in discourse was evident in the consistent replacement of the word 'women' by 'parent' (SOU 1972:34, pp 17-44). This signalled that the insurance would now be gender-neutral: support would no longer be aimed at women only, but should instead give both parents the opportunity to take responsibility for taking care of their children. The aim was to give 'parents themselves the right to decide which one of them should stay at home and take care of the child' (SOU 1972:34, p 45).

The reform proposal did not end there. The new parental insurance was composed of several different layers. The first would be a guarantee level, to all parents, irrespective of income and employment. Fathers would be guaranteed 10 days of paid leave in conjunction with childbirth. The sickness insurance would cover income losses when one of the parents stayed at home with sick children. Parents with seriously disabled children would be eligible for 'caring support', conditions for foster parents and adoptive parents would be equal to those of biological parents within the social insurance system, and single parents would also be covered on the same terms as married couples (SOU 1972:34, p 45 onwards).

The motive behind the proposed change was the perceived need for the modernisation of family policy:

> The development of society leads to new demands from families on the design of economic support. The development towards increasing equality between men and women in society and in family life, which among other things makes it less justified to base social legislation on a 'sole provider' in the family, is probably the most striking example of the changes that influence the preconditions for family support. (SOU 1972:34, p 199)

The directives to the commission proceeded from the established idea that family policy should serve as a means to equalise conditions between families with and without children, and between small and large families with children.

The principle that justice, social redistribution and freedom of choice, rather than population policy, should guide family policy was reconfirmed. The emphasis on freedom of choice was important, as it united the political parties in parliament, although it was founded on an ambiguous gender dimension. The political ambition to increase the father's participation in family life by the end of the 1960s, which was an important part of the parental insurance scheme, was also an important arena for the construction of the new 'daddy role', that is, a father who had gainful employment and took care of his children (Klinth, 2002, p 200). Gender-equal relations, then, came to be about women's right to work and economic freedom, and men's right to an active family life – so-called double emancipation. However, the gender-equal policy process, which had guided the development of gender-neutral parental insurance reform, came to be conditional; the father's right to use the parental insurance had become a free choice, while the mother's use of the parental insurance was seen as something natural and necessary. This led to a development where women are still seen as the main carer of the family, despite a reverse ambition for gender equality (Åström, 1990; SOU 2005:66).

The commission called for a flexible design of family support, as family forms and functions change over time – children grow up, spouses may divorce and so on. Family policy should accommodate transitions of family structures and social conditions in general. Three such changes were emphasised in particular. The first was the growing number of women in the labour market, and the accompanying changes in the economic regulation of families (for instance, the individual taxation system). The second was the prolonged education of children and young adults, and the third was the impact of immigration:

> Sweden has become an immigrant country. Immigrant children
> are ... a group whose size is approaching the group of children in
> single-parent families (8-9%). It is important both for the families
> themselves and for the entire society that these families are given
> similar possibilities to give their children a good home environment
> and that they are not isolated in certain housing districts.... It is
> important that they can benefit from the same support as Swedish
> families in similar circumstances, without delays and discrimination.
> (SOU 1972:34, p 202)

'Immigrant children' should therefore be treated on equal terms with 'Swedish children', a paradoxical combination of equality and difference that will be addressed in the final chapter of this book. Hence, the ambition to avoid the segregation between 'Swedish families' and 'immigrant families' was an important goal of family policy (and therefore, indirectly, created segregation between the two by emphasising the specific position of immigrants).

Perhaps the major object of reform was men within the family sphere. In a direct break with the received wisdom of family policy so far, the commission did not separate the roles of women and men even in the earliest phases of children's lives. Men were as important as women right from the time of birth, and family policy should therefore not discriminate between women and men on the basis of biological differences, traditional notions of responsibilities and so on (SOU 1972:34, p 224).

Another key ambition was to support low-income families, a goal that again was widely embraced and that did not meet with political resistance within the commission. The only area where some controversy emerged concerned so-called caring support or, later on, cash-for-care schemes (*vårdnadsbidrag*). While conservatives and liberals in the commission were in favour of supporting those families where one parent stayed at home with the children, the majority opposed it, for financial reasons and because of the alleged negative impact on gender equality.

The gender-neutral parental insurance scheme was established in 1974, replacing gender-specific maternity insurance. It gave both fathers and mothers the right to childcare support, so as to make it easier for women to go out to work. In its parliamentary Bill, the government adopted the commission's proposal for two-tier parental insurance. The basic level was set at 25 kronor per day irrespective of previous income and employment, while the second tier covered a period of 180 days (seven months) and compensated for 90% of previously earned income. Income from parental insurance was taxed and qualified for the supplementary pension system.

Immediately after parental insurance was established, a new commission was appointed, this time to evaluate the impact of the insurance and to investigate the question of whether the insurance should be allocated by quotas (SOU 1978:38). Nothing came out of this, but yet another commission proposed a system with five months of parental support, shared between parents to enable a reduction in working hours A system of this kind was established in 1978, when the insurance expanded to cover a period of 12 months (of which nine months compensated for 90% of previously earned income).

'Children in a softer society'

While much of the discussion about families concerned women and men in the household and in the labour market (and at the interstices between the two), the role of children (as family members and as citizens in the society of the future) was becoming a growing family policy concern during the 1970s. It was not only children's social conditions in general that concerned the public commissions, but also the interplay between children's development and the array of public institutions for childcare. The intellectual foundations of the commissions' studies of children's conditions in contemporary society came from the fields of developmental psychology, social psychology and educational research (SOU 1972:26 and 27; SOU 1975:31; SOU 1975:33; SOU 1975:35; SOU 1975:37; SOU 1975:39). Many of these were research reports without a mandate to present policy proposals, but this did not prevent them from having considerable impact.

At the time, Prime Minister Olof Palme had initiated a discourse on the 'softer society', where system reforms would be complemented by a greater concern for the human dimensions of society and the living conditions of children and adults in the welfare state. The endurance of the discourse showed itself after the election in 1976, when the centre-right government proclaimed, in wording resembling that of its social democratic predecessor, that:

> The goal of family policy is to create a good environment for children to grow up in and social security for families with children. Family policy should also be designed to support equality between women and men. Various family policy measures should give families with children increasing possibilities to live on the same social and economic terms as other groups. Family support in the form of child allowances, housing allowance and parental insurance reduces the economic strains of having and raising children. Expanded social services, for instance in child-care, create the practical possibilities for children and parents alike to develop as individuals and as members of an increasingly complicated society. (Bill 1978/79, no. 168, pp 18-19)

Returning to the period of social democratic rule, its change in policy discourse was, not surprisingly, accompanied by a government commission, the childhood environment commission. The commission was to conduct a scientific survey of living conditions for children, including their health, development and care, as well as the impact of changes in working life and housing (SOU 1975:30, p 288).

Many of these reports were produced within the framework of the commission; while primarily serving as surveys of research in their respective fields, they also functioned as ideological beacons and as avant-garde proposals. For instance, in one of the reports, the sociologist Rita Liljeström proclaimed that modern life had resulted in deep divisions, even conflicts, between families and society. With industrialisation, interrelated activities had become differentiated and now formed separate social systems. Furthermore, social networks based on informal contacts between individuals in the local community had been replaced by impersonal social policy measures aimed at universal and accessible welfare protection. In lieu of dense social networks, families affected by geographical mobility, urbanisation and industrial transformation developed defensive mechanisms and joined together against a – purportedly – hostile environment. This, Liljeström argued, had a particularly negative impact on children, who experienced feelings of insecurity and weakened self-development when they left the comfort of their homes (SOU 1975:31, p 23).

Liljeström did not express any nostalgic sentiments. She stressed that the reforms taken had been justified by the need to develop welfare and combat poverty. She did, however, point to the values that been lost in the societal transformation, as social networks 'took shape within the framework of poverty and constant struggles against destitution' but life forms, she argued, 'were local and constant' (SOU 1975:31, p 27).

The report emphasised that the gendered division of labour had a long history, preceding the industrial revolution, but accentuated by the normative focus on the nuclear family in the post-war period. While the fixed roles of women and men were increasingly under pressure, not least because of the growing number of women participating in the labour market, the sanctity of motherhood nevertheless remained a starting point for the everyday life of women and men, and for social reform. Rita Liljeström was part of a re-evaluation of motherhood in her critique of biological (and psycho-analytical) theories of maternal deprivation: 'I would almost wish to say that a child is born twice, first biologically – and then the mother is irreplaceable – and six months later socially, and then other people who care about the child are equally capable. The capacity for love is not a biological but a social quality' (SOU 1975:31, p 80).

Liljeström drew attention to the ambiguities in contemporary society. Efficiency and rationality were cherished, but motherhood and reproduction were romanticised, locking women into a function which could readily be shared between women and men: 'While the economic and political sectors of society have triggered rationality further and further, the institutions related to reproduction indulge in ever more fatalism, irrationality and sensuality' (SOU 1975:31, p 96). Gender relations lagged behind in the modernisation of society, which had hitherto focused primarily on material conditions. The result was a strange hybrid of biological understanding of gender and nostalgic reaction against rationality. Liljeström's suggested remedy was a constructivist approach to gender and caring, where roles and tasks were negotiated rather than fixed. In a later text, Liljeström also promoted a model of shared roles, where the dual-earner, care-sharing family ought to be promoted by a strong and active welfare state (Liljeström, 1978).

A commission makes a wish

Liljeström's influence was evident in other reports from the childhood environment commission. In one of these, the impact of labour markets on children's development was scrutinised. The tone was alarmist:

> Because of the length and location of working hours, and the time spent commuting, many parents do not find sufficient time to spend with their children. Many parents are so physically and mentally exhausted after work that they do not have the energy to be with their children. The statements of many parents are evidence of this. The time for children is often short and without quality. It is obvious that today's working life as a whole is detrimental to families and their children. Working hours, work environment, the nature of work, work commuting, etc must be changed to fit better with the way humans live, the way children live. (SOU 1975:37, p 49)

What was needed, the report concluded, was a radical overhaul of social and economic conditions, incidentally not unrelated to what actually came into being in the coming decade – shortened and more flexible working hours, co-determination at the workplace, an expansion of social services, legally enforced gender equality in the labour market and so on. Altogether, this would give parents more time to spend with their children and to do so with the responsibility shared jointly between women and men (SOU 1975:37, p 126).

Hence, the commission had a plethora of radical proposals to consider. It embraced their visionary elements, reaching the conclusion that it was 'not possible to create a good living environment for children without creating a good society for all, based on the right to work for everyone, an even distribution of wealth, production for the needs of the majority of the people, and a fair distribution of influence over it all, but also over the individual life situation' (SOU 1975:30, p 277).

Reforms directed towards the living conditions of children could therefore, the commission concluded, focus on a broader set of policies, in particular those that relate to the interface between working life and parenthood. The list that the commission was presented with ranged from shortened working hours, improved social and physical conditions in childcare and schooling, and a more humane orientation of housing policies, with low, dense housing rather than high-rise buildings.

The reports from the childhood environment commission primarily functioned as visionary projections and ideological beacons; the commission presented little in the way of proposals that were ready for implementation. There were, however, some concrete suggestions that supported the role and position of children in society. One concerned so-called parental education, proposed by a government commission on childcare (SOU 1978:5). In effect, universal – but not compulsory – parental education was established in 1980, run by the county councils in conjunction with maternity care and childcare (Bill 1978/79, no. 168).

A children-friendly society could only be devised by parents together with their children; this, in turn, called for increasing knowledge about the needs and conditions of children among parents. Part of this could be fulfilled by parental education, guiding new parents into a more secure role in a society where social relations had become much more frail, where families were becoming smaller and where family life and working life had been separated. Tensions pertaining to 'immigrant parents' were also discussed at length, and the government acknowledged – while pushing hard for the integration of non-Swedish parents – the drawbacks of forced assimilation and the risk of a social and cultural clash between 'immigrant parents' and Swedish society and social norms (Bill 1978/79, no. 168, p 26; see also Hammar, 1999 and Dahlström, 2004 and for a further and more comprehensive analysis of immigration policies at the time). It was clear that the government wanted to reach immigrant groups with its educational plans, and earmarked resources were allocated to county councils and immigrant organisations to develop study materials, employ interpreters, and design courses specifically for immigrants. In doing so, the government – as it acknowledged – was pursuing a fine line; the ambition was not to assimilate immigrants, but it was important that the material conveyed information about 'Swedish conditions'. Immigrants were offered the opportunity to participate in the same parental educational programmes as Swedish parents, but if the language barrier was considered to be too great, education was to be offered in other languages as well.

Hence, separation and integration formed an uneasy alliance in the government's stance on the education of 'immigrant parents'. While the government's motivation ostensibly concerned language comprehension, a cultural ambiguity was also evident in its approach: should all groups in society be included on equal terms or should education be tailor-made for different groups?

'The goal is gender equality'

The United Nations declared 1975 International Women's Year. The countries of the world were urged to establish equality commissions to study the situation of women and suggest measures to improve their conditions. Sweden adopted the recommendation and appointed a commission that worked on the basis of three principles: the integration of gender equality within the broader area of social and economic equality; everybody's right to work; and equal access to democratic participation. An attempt was thereby taking place to integrate gender equality as a policy field and as an integral part of existing reform strands rather than a separate policy field.

In a summary of the impact of gender equality reforms, some observations were made on the status of gender equality in Sweden:

- fewer children born but with shorter intervals than in the 1930s and 1940s;
- increased life expectancy for both women and men;
- easier domestic labour;
- a reduction in working hours;
- an increase in the educational levels of women;
- a constant increase in the demand for female labour;
- improved knowledge and understanding of the needs of children to have contact with their fathers and with other children;
- a growing awareness of the constructed rather than biological foundation of gender (sex) roles (SOU 1975:58, p 16).

While cherishing the progress made, the report highlighted continuing problems. One of these was the shortage of childcare places and another was the organisation of households. If gender equality were to be attained, it was necessary to bring about a new division of labour 'based on solidarity and equality in working life and in the homes' (SOU 1975:58, p 10). Only then would the combination of gainful employment and caring become an asset rather than a burden. Employers and employment conditions also played a pivotal role, as shorter working hours for parents with small children were necessary steps on the road to gender equality. Another difficulty was the uneven connection to the labour market among women and men – women worked fewer hours with lower salaries than men and their contribution was less valued.

> In earlier times, it was considered natural that the conflict between children and gainful employment was a concern for women and in particular single mothers. Various solutions as to how to protect the role of the mother and to enable the family to live on one income – the man's – were discussed. Now the orientation is different, with double roles for both parents. Instead of a choice between home and children (for women) and gainful employment (for men), the current discourse is that it is positive for all people to have the right to have double roles, both as employed and as an active parent. The double role has often been placed on women, making it rather heavy to bear. Therefore, there is a growing awareness that men must take increasing responsibilities for household and children…. (SOU 1975:58, pp 62-3)

What is evident in this account, and rather typical of the time, is a focus on individuals in interaction – women, men and children – that radically departed from the discourse just a decade earlier, when the family was being portrayed as a unified and coherent object. The family is seen as a nexus of relationships, not only personal but also institutional, as working life, social services, education and socioeconomic policies all had a major impact on individuals and their relationships within the family. Hence, the family was being 'deconstructed' and the tensions between different roles and positions, social and ethnic backgrounds were acknowledged rather than disguised or neglected, as in earlier accounts. Not surprisingly, the intellectual influences no longer came from structural-functionalist accounts but rather from women's studies and from more open-ended research in social psychology, psychology, education and the sociology of the interplay between individuals and society.

While the tone of the discourse was critical, it was also optimistic. In due course, and with all forces joined, a good and equal society could be built. Sweden had come a long way, and by the year 2000 inequality would be eradicated. At least, this was the expectation and explicit hope for the future.

The law on gender equality

In the 1970s, gender equality as a concept and as a family life practice had been institutionalised, although it had to compete for political and public attention with the other reform project of the decade – gender equality and democratisation in working life (Hirdman, 1990; Acker et al, 1992). These two projects were often blended – the key to gender equality in society and within the family was, it was argued, a reformed working life. It was not only a matter of women's right to work – that, it was argued, had already been achieved – but improvements were also needed in the interface between the household and the labour market. The expressions of political will took shape first in agreements in the state sector and later also in the private sector. In 1979, a law on gender equality was proposed by the minority liberal government (in office from 1978-79), on the basis of suggestions from a government commission on gender equality. The proposed law was intended to serve the purpose of protecting the individual against discrimination on the basis of gender (SOU 1978:38). By purportedly addressing the conditions of women and men in the labour market, and their equal rights to work and sustainable working conditions, the government intended to break down the gender segregation in the labour market and accelerate gender equality (Bill 1978/79, no. 175, p 22).

The Bill placed the primary responsibility for promoting gender equality in the workplace on the labour market parties in line with the tradition of voluntary agreements (rather than legislation). Nonetheless, the employers were assigned the lead role, carrying out the task of creating gender balance in the workplace and actively recruiting staff of 'underrepresented gender'. An equality ombudsman and an equality board were to be appointed, to supervise the development of gender equality in the labour market by means of information and campaigning, but also direct interventions in companies and other workplaces.

The intention was for the equality board to be made up of representatives with particular knowledge about gender relations in the labour market and key actors from within the labour market parties – hence, the ambition was again to balance the focus on gender with the needs of labour market (Bill 1978/79, no. 175, p 3).

The Liberal Party had formed an extreme minority government, holding only 39 of the 349 seats in parliament. Some of its proposals did not pass and the final decision focused on sex discrimination only. Equality in the workplace was relegated to the labour market parties, leaving only the fields not governed by collective bargaining within the remit of the equality ombudsman and the equality board.

While the gender equality Act may seem like the climax of a long period of gender equality regulation, much was still to be done. Women still worked fewer hours than men on average, and took the main bulk of responsibility for childcare and the household. This shaped the family policy agenda of the coming decade(s).

Conclusion

Gender, care and work in the welfare state

In the early 1960s, influential debaters like Eva Moberg argued that the very foundations of gender relations would have to change if gender equality were ever to be achieved. Women's ability to give birth was not to be equated with the ability to care; caring for and raising children was therefore a task to be shared between the father and the mother. If such a division of caring responsibilities were realised, women and men would be equals in the labour market and in society more generally. This opened up the space for the radicalisation of family policy.

The debate was further intensified with the advent of Scandinavian 'sex-role research', which in its turn shaped the emerging debate on 'sex roles'. This concept had by this time migrated from social scientific discourse to policy debates. The sex-role debate was the impetus to transform family politics and change the discourse on women and men, families and labour market participants, the role of the state in regulating family affairs and socialisation patterns. Gender equality, care and work became intertwined entities – the gendered care work.

The structural development in the labour market opened another window of opportunity for the transformation of gender relations. The long period of economic growth and the increasing labour shortages of the 1960s led to an increased search for new labour sources; married women and housewives, together with immigrants, became an increasingly important 'reserve army' of labour, in the late 1960s in particular. Prevailing views on women as the 'caring heads' of the family were questioned, not only by feminists and radical social scientists but also by the labour market parties and mainstream politicians. In the wake of this debate, the stay-at-home housewife and the male-breadwinner model were increasingly undermined when the ideological critique was combined with structural measures to increase the supply of labour. This made way for the rise of a weak male-breadwinner model (Jane Lewis, 1997, 2001) – when larger numbers of women entered the labour market, public day care expanded and the social security system was individualised. Thus, women were no longer the sole targets for family policy reforms. The notion of the caring father emerged in the policy discourse, as did the idea of shared responsibilities between women and men. With Rita Liljeström's (1978) (and others') re-evaluation of motherhood, the construction of masculinity and femininity was transformed not only in the eyes of the intellectuals but also in those of the policymakers. Moreover, the real breakthrough for gender neutrality came with the individualisation of the social policy system and in the emergence of what Helga Hernes (1987) referred to as the notion of a 'women-friendly' welfare state.

Gender equality, gender neutrality and the individualisation of the family

By introducing gender neutrality as a means to achieve gender equality, previous patterns in family policy development were broken, and the former family policy paradox was resolved in policy discourse. Following the sex-role debate and the rise of social justice and freedom to choose as political catchphrases, the notion of the 'gender-equal family' emerged. The gender equality discourse centred around women's right to work and their economic freedom but also men's right to parenthood and to partake in an active family life (double emancipation).

The gender-equal family ideal was backed by several actors – by the labour market parties in their attempts to include women in the workforce, by the women's movement in its ambition to empower women, and by the political parties, not least the social democrats, in their ambition to sharpen their political edge by embracing gender equality.

One major step towards establishing a gender-neutral ideal of family policy was taken at the Social Democratic Party congress in 1969. Here, it was argued that inequalities were a characteristic not only of gender relations, but also of general social conditions, in Sweden and globally. The ensuing recommendation for the labour movement was to embrace equality as a leading ideological theme. All policy fields were to be included: labour market policy, social policy, housing policy, educational policy, consumer policy, legal policy, and wage and tax policies. The purported goal was no less than a classless society. Arguably, this was a first attempt to introduce what later became known as 'gender mainstreaming', although the term equality at this time included both class and gender relations.

In this all-embracing ambition, family policy was aimed at abolishing traditional 'sex roles'. Not only should the roles of men and women be transformed, but also traditional views of femininity and masculinity should be challenged. Moreover, it was argued that if true equality was to be achieved, the focal object for social reforms had to be the *adult individual*. This would entail a revision of family laws (inheritance and marriage), social and labour market policy and the tax system (individual taxation). This would make all social insurances gender-neutral and based on individual incomes.

The paradox resurfaced. While individuals should be freed from traditional sex roles and family dependencies, the nuclear family was still cherished as a source of stability in a changing world. But it was a somewhat different nuclear family that was outlined, one composed of autonomous but interrelated individuals. The vision was, as mentioned earlier, a classless society where (individual) women and men would live under equal conditions. If this was to be realised within the constraints of the nuclear family, the division between a male breadwinner and a female carer had to be replaced by an integrated model of caring *and* working fathers and mothers.

However, this debate was pursued not only among social democrats, but also among liberals and within the Communist Party. The debate flourished in the media and in the new women's movement. Hence, the change in family policy was broadly embraced.

In the aftermath of the intense debates of the 1960s came a string of reforms with a gender-neutral focus. In 1970, 'housewife insurance' was made gender-neutral and, a year later, individual taxation was introduced, labelled at the time the 'greatest equality reform ever'. Maternity insurance was replaced with a gender-neutral parental insurance scheme in 1973, and the marriage Act was changed so that the father could apply for child custody after a divorce.

By the mid-1970s, the international economic crisis had reached Sweden and the Swedish model was slowly undermined. Family policy reforms also changed direction in the 1970s, from a focus on equal relations within the families to one on gender equality in a wider context, in particular gender equality in the labour market, in what was possibly the greatest political project of the decade. Its showcase was the gender equality Act, which promoted anti-discrimination in the labour market. This was to be heavily debated in the decades to come.

Note

[1] I have not carried out an in-depth analysis of the women's movement and its significance for family policy development. This development has been well documented, for example, in Dahlerup, 1998; Karlsson, 2001; Schmitz, 2007.

FIVE

Family policy in the age of neoliberalism

This chapter turns to the evolution of family policy in an era marked by the contraction of the state, erratic economic growth and cuts in welfare services. Developments in family policy (and social policy in general) had formerly been shaped by seemingly endless economic growth, creating a manoeuvring space for ambitious reformers. Around 1980, however, the era of big reforms and the ever-expanding state seemed to be over. The corporatist decision-making model and the bureaucratic state came under increasing fire. One of the many facets of corporatism was the system of public commissions as a means of surveying areas of potential political intervention and preparing policy reforms. With the pressure on public finances building, the consensus-building public commissions were waning in impact, while the very idea of ever-increasing political intervention was increasingly questioned. These combined factors signalled a change in Swedish political culture, as consensus and long-term deliberations were discarded in favour of a much more conflictual political style, emphasising speed and efficiency rather than broad consultation.

The changing ideological tide impinged on family policy, although in a different direction and form from policy elsewhere in the political landscape. Feminist research challenged dominant beliefs about caring responsibilities and gender roles, as did the emerging field of men's studies. During the 1980s and 1990s, the government appointed a number of so-called men's groups that based their work on research into men and masculinity. Feminist research also changed; following the trend in international debates, women's studies reinvented itself as gender studies and encompassed an increasingly complex and advanced analysis of gender relations. This complexity also spilled over into political debates about the family.

During this period, gender equality policy more or less subsumed family policy. Family policy measures were just one of many parts in the presentation of gender equality goals. The family as an entity, and as a group, had waned in significance and the political discourse instead referred to the experience of individual women and men. This policy development resonated in the theoretical work of Anthony Giddens and Ulrich Beck, among others, on the individualisation process. Without necessarily referring to individualisation as a laudable goal, family policy came to address the conditions for the individual in post-industrial society. The transformation of family policy coincided with the ascent of neoliberalism, even though neoliberalism in its Swedish incarnation was truncated, leading one observer, the geographer David Harvey, to label it 'circumscribed neoliberalisation': 'The public still remained broadly attached to its welfare structures. Inequality certainly increased, but by no means to the levels seen in the US or the UK. Poverty levels remained low and levels of social provision remained high' (Harvey, 2005, p 115).

Circumscribed neoliberalism shaped family policy, too, although in a paradoxical and somewhat incoherent fashion, with individualisation and reflexive flexibility at one extreme and the structural subordination of women at the other, coexisting and not without tension. Both these positions referred back to earlier phases of gender-equality policy – the former a reflection of the defamiliarisation that began in the 1960s, the latter an extrapolation of the 'sex-role debate' and the durability of the social categories of the same decade. The resulting incoherence between individualisation and structuralism came to shape much of the family policy paradox over the period. Moreover, the remit of gender-equality policy expanded and by the mid-1990s the gender policy goals were included in, and were supposed to influence, all policy areas ('gender mainstreaming').

Some more singular events also shaped family policy in the period. At the beginning of the 1990s, the so-called Support Stockings (Stödstrumporna – a play on words, recalling the Redstockings of the women's liberation movement and the Swedish term for compression stockings) was formed as a pressure group to increase the number of women in prominent public posts, their position being that if the political parties did not heed their demands, they would campaign for a women's party (opinion polls had indicated that roughly 15% of the vote at the time would go such a party). The impact was felt immediately and after the election of 1994 half of MPs were women (Törnqvist, 2006).

The 1990s witnessed continual radicalisation where unequal relations were understood as a reflection of power relations between the genders. This radicalisation – shaped by a profound influence from academic and political feminism – culminated in the first half of the 2000s. In 2001, the Social Democratic Party declared itself a feminist party (the Left Party had already declared itself feminist in 1996) and a few years later (2005) a new party with an explicit feminist orientation, Feminist Initiative (F!), was formed.

This period was therefore dramatic and varied both in ideological terms and in terms of the very organisation of Swedish post-war society in the form of a political-economic compact that came to be called 'the Swedish model'. It is to these changes that we now turn.

Dismantling the welfare state

The social democrats came to power in 1982 after six years of bourgeois government, with a programme emphasising that the recovery of the economy should be export- and investment-led. The programme referred to itself as a 'third way' between monetarism and Keynesianism (Benner, 1997). The 'big bang' currency devaluation of 16% was the cornerstone of the new political and crisis strategy. The profit regulation of the Rehn-Meidner model, it was argued, was no longer viable. Instead, profit *as such* had to be the target of labour movement programmes. The novelty of the 'third way' was its explicit orientation to corporate profitability and the expectation that other elements in economic and labour market regulation would adhere to this target.

The 'third way', however, turned out to be a failure, resulting in high inflation, wage increases higher than those of Sweden's trading partners and the organisational disintegration of the industrial relations system. Moreover, a more ideological motive seems to have been to weaken LO and its connection to the Social Democratic Party, thereby paving the way for a 'system shift' in Swedish politics. Neoliberalism had entered the political stage and political development during the 1990s was indeed marked by this shift in perspective (Rothstein and Bergström, 1999).

In 1991, a centre-right government took power, comprising four parties – the Liberal Party, the Centre Party, the Christian Democratic Party and the Moderate Party – and headed by Carl Bildt of the Moderate Party. Its main rhetoric was for a 'new start for Sweden' and a revolution in the 'freedom to choose' (as opposed to the alleged rigidity of welfare service provision hitherto). This ideological shift was most obvious in the provision of social services, for example the introduction of a voucher system in schools and hospitals.

However, when it came to economic policy making, the government was not in a situation to make any radical moves. It continued its predecessor's hard currency policy, which met with massive currency speculations at the beginning of 1992 and led to the Swedish krona being floated in late 1992 (leading to a *de facto* 20% devaluation). When the hard currency policy failed – and unemployment rose from 1.5% to 9% in just a few years – the government instead aimed to reduce the public deficit and lower inflation. As a result, the government reduced compensation rates and sickness, parental and unemployment insurance to 80% (from 90%). This decision led to a parliamentary crisis and an agreement was reached with the social democrats on a common policy based on saving (Benner, 1997).

The economic crisis and mass unemployment led to failure for the conservative government in the 1994 election. The new social democratic government adopted a policy based on the conviction that reduced budget deficits would lead to lower interest rates that, in turn, would stimulate economic growth and employment. The strategy was later described by its chief architect and later Prime Minister, Göran Persson, as an 'accountant's strategy'. This strategy also included further cuts to social insurance, down to 75%. In addition, child allowance was reduced and the supplementary support for large families was abolished (Benner and Vad, 2000).

The 1998 election was a disaster for the social democrats, who had their worst election result since 1920 (36.6% of the votes). Nevertheless, it was able to form a new government with the support of the Green Party and the Left Party. This government continued to dismantle the public sector through massive reductions in social services, especially through lower state support to municipalities and county councils, leading to job losses mainly in the female-dominated health sector (Benner and Vad, 2000). As a result, fertility rates decreased rapidly – in

1990 women gave birth to 2.1 babies a year on average, but by 1999 this number had fallen to 1.5 (Stanfors, 2007).

Thus, the period was marked by severe economic crisis as well as the dismantling of the welfare state, and economic policy making – its discourse, practices and consequences – was thoroughly transformed between 1980 and 2000. These changes affected family policy in direction and discourse.

Family policy between feminist research and gender equality policy

The 'sex-role debate' had influenced the gender equality discourse of the 1970s, when policy goals were formulated in neutral terms such as 'children's need', 'parents' need' or 'everyone's need' for equality. Differences in social conditions of men and women were generally downplayed, but they returned to the forefront of policy debate in the 1980s (Roman, 2008).

The change in policy discourse manifested itself in two government commissions (SOU 1979:89; SOU 1982:18). Both made critical evaluations of the family and equality policies pursued in the 1970s, as all evidence showed that women still shouldered the bulk of responsibilities for children and the household, to the detriment of their life situation and their position within working life. Gender equality policy had failed, the commissions concluded, at least from the perspective of women. They also criticised the gender-neutral laws and regulations that had been enacted; they were seen as powerless as long as women had a more vulnerable position in the labour market (SOU 1982:18). As a response to the critique, the social democratic government presented an action list to improve women's conditions in the labour market, the primary aim being to improve levels of education but also through a survey of women's representation in public policy making and policy advice (Bill 1984/85, no. 130). A government commission was appointed for the latter, and its 1987 report, *Roundabout with the Ladies* (*Varannan damernas*) (SOU 1987:19), is discussed later.

The lacklustre impact of gender equality policy until the early 1980s can partly be explained by the economic crisis of the 1970s, which circumscribed the manoeuvring space for reformist policies. The commissions of the 1960s had afforded major reforms to bring about a change from a single-household (male-breadwinner) model to a dual-income model. Fifteen years later, this vision had become reality. Now came the second phase of family reforms, namely to comprehend the consequences of this shift for families in general and women in particular – had genuine gender equality really been established? The relative discontent was further articulated by a new generation of feminist researchers, who argued that women's and men's interests were not always congruent, and that political determination was necessary to bring about gender equality (Florin and Karlsson, 2000; Roman, 2008).

The two new commissions set up to examine family and equality policies were influenced by the emerging feminist perspectives on gender relations. Both put women's situation foremost. For the first time ever in Swedish gender equality policy, men were pinpointed as the primary source of inequality within families. By withdrawing from their responsibilities for children and household, they had relegated women to a secondary position in society: 'Women's dependence on child-care and their weaker position in working life largely stem from men's lack of engagement in family tasks' (SOU 1979:89, p 31). At the same time, the commission highlighted the economic and social value of unpaid labour in the household, drawing on ongoing feminist debates on the importance of household work (compare Oakley, 1974; Molyneux, 1979; see also Roman, 2008, Lundqvist and Roman, 2008).

Men as a group were held responsible for women's subordination in the labour market. It was their reluctance to take part in childcare and housework that had locked women into a secondary position in the labour market. This in turn led to a critique of mere lip service to the goals of equality in the household and within the family, as little had been done in reality to entice men to spend more time with their children or work in the household. Parental insurance was an example of one step that had been taken in this direction, formally giving fathers equal rights to stay at home with small children, but in fact it had done little to alter gender relations within families (Widerberg, 1981, 1986; Åström, 1990). Women took the bulk of parental leave, leading to a clash between the gender policy rhetoric of shared parenthood between women and men and gender policy practice, where in fact 'parent' equalled 'mother' (Åström, 1990).

Against the background of this critique, a working group was appointed in 1983 with a mandate to analyse and transform men's role in work for gender equality. A gender equality council was also established, with which the working group collaborated on awareness raising among men. In a report entitled *Man in Transition*, (*Mannen i förändring*, 1985) the working group presented several proposals to strengthen awareness of gender equality among men. Parental insurance was to be developed further and shared equally; men were to be involved and included in maternity and paediatric healthcare to a greater extent; and family counselling and therapy were to be offered to men to help them change their marital habits. It was also recommended that men should receive more support after divorce, and be encouraged to take more responsibility for children after a separation. All of these became recurrent themes in family policy in the following decade, when 'daddy politics' became one of its dominant themes (Bergman and Hobson, 2002; Hobson, 2002). A steady stream of studies of men and fathers appeared, and seldom before had the situation of men been so closely scrutinised. In doing so, it was hoped to explain the origins of violence, family absence, poor health and men's unwillingness to make use of parental insurance (Klinth, 2002, p 309).

Roundabout with the Ladies

Roundabout with the Ladies (SOU 1987:19) addressed the mounting critique of gender equality policy and its meagre impact. In short, its remedy was to propose the sharing of power, influence and responsibilities between women and men, primarily through gender quotas in the public sector. The commission anticipated the traditional critique of such measures, arguing that gender equality should be achieved through voluntary measures rather than by fiat, but took the criticism lightly:

> We have shown with a large number of examples that conditions are different for women and men. We therefore ask ourselves what impact gender-neutral measures have in a society which is not gender-neutral. We have also concluded that, in practice, a contradiction often occurs between equality and 'democracy'. Equality as a political principle seems to be applicable only when it is not in contradiction with other principles. We argue instead that democracy increases with gender equality. We also argue the voluntary road is no longer viable. So far, this road has not led to gender equality even though the possibility for this has been there at all times, and even more so now considering that it now enjoys the support of laws and regulations. The voluntary road is not viable if the goal is to be achieved within the foreseeable future. (SOU 1987:19, p 42)

Hence, the commission proposed legislation on equal representation on the boards of government agencies by 1998, with interim targets set for 1992 (30%) and 1995 (40%). While its immediate impact was limited, the commission's report sparked off a debate that, among other things, contributed to the formation of the Support Stockings feminist network. The group was very active in the debates preceding the 1991 election, in which gender representation became a major issue (Törnqvist, 2006). By demanding 'half the power and full salary', Support Stockings managed to bring gender dimensions into the political election campaign arena. It has thus been claimed that gender as a political dimension first became visible through *Roundabout with the Ladies* and the following debate (Åström, 1990; Landby Eduards & Åström, 1993; Törnqvist, 2006), Hence, even though its immediate impact was limited, and the proposed gender quota system was rejected, it had major long-term consequences, as female representation was increasingly embraced by all political parties.

The five-year plan

Rejecting gender quotas, the government proceeded on the voluntary path, manifested most clearly in the gender equality Bill presented in 1987. Drawing on *Roundabout with the Ladies* in its analysis of the state of gender equality in

Sweden, it nevertheless prescribed less radical remedies for the future. It located the main thrust of forthcoming reforms in the areas of labour market and education policies, arguing that the gender-segregated labour market was the main obstacle to equality in working life and within the family (Bill 1987/88, no. 105).

The Bill, *Goals for Gender Equality Policy*, continued on the well-trodden path of gender equality and family policy reforms, where women's employment patterns were the key to enhanced gender equality. Women had a similar right to gainful employment as men, an ideal that had shaped employment regulation in the post-war period; the co-determination law, the expansion of social insurances in general and parental insurance in particular, and the safeguarding of part-time work had all served to enhance the position of women in the labour market. In addition, the labour market parties had agreed in 1960 to abandon 'women's salaries', with the effect that income differences between women and men were narrowing. This led the social democratic government to conclude that the gender equality policy pursued so far had been successful. However, some critical issues remained to be addressed. Many of the goals had not been attained; the labour market was still highly gender-segregated, and women could be found in the areas and occupations with the lowest salaries and with the most monotonous and repetitive workloads. Women's share of employment varied considerably between different parts of the country, and involuntary part-time work was much more frequent for women than for men. Educational choice was still highly gender-specific, with girls dominating in education for caring occupations and boys in technical education. Household work and childcare were still predominantly female responsibilities, and women adjusted their working patterns to reflect this. In the mid-1980s, 83% of women between 25 and 44 years of age participated in the labour market, and more than half of them worked part time (in the mid-1980s, 96% of all men participated in the labour market and 3% of them worked part time). It was feared that the situation would be further aggravated by an ageing population, as without an expansion of state care for the elderly, women would probably also bear the brunt of this responsibility (Bill 1987/88, no. 105). As the situation threatened to become polarised, the government expressed the fear that turning ideological tides would reverse the progress made:

> There are also some contemporary tendencies which, if not actively fought, may lead to a contraction within the field of gender equality. Neo-liberal reasoning on the public support of privatisation of different areas means, in reality, that resources will be withdrawn from the public sector, which may lead to lowered quality in child-care, health care and education. This in its turn may become a motive for well-to-do groups to search for private solutions, which would increase class differences in society. Parents would then no longer be able to trust that their children are in a safe and developing environment while they themselves are working or studying. (Bill 1987/88, no. 105, p 7)

The long-term goals of gender equality policy were repeated in the Bill: women and men should have equal responsibilities, obligations and possibilities, irrespective of area. Equal relations were defined as a situation where 'each and everyone has a job which is paid sufficiently for their own subsistence, [where] women and men share the responsibility for children and housework, and [where] both genders engage as much in politics, union affairs, and other common matters in working life and society' (Bill 1987/88, no. 105, p 30).

In connection with the policy choices of earlier periods, gender equality policy was interwoven with other political areas, in particular with labour market policy but also with economic policy more generally. Gender equality could therefore not be distinguished from the broader political project of diminishing socioeconomic divisions.

Children and their rights were also included in the gender equality policy mix, reflecting the fact that the conditions of upbringing were part of the equality goals. The discussion primarily focused on the labour market, and how women and men could manage the precarious balance between parenthood and gainful employment. The solution envisaged was increasing investments in state childcare, even though such measures had to be coupled with a new view of maleness and radical reforms of work organisation to have a major impact on gender equality (Bill 1987/88, no. 105).

Summarising its ambitions, the government presented a five-year action plan for gender equality in 1988. The first goal was economic independence and economic equality, which were identified as the key factors in gender equality policy. Income differences should diminish, as should the gender income gap. The second target was equality in the labour market and the uneven distribution of household work. At the time, only four out of 52 occupational fields were gender-balanced. Inspired by *Roundabout with the Ladies*, the goal was set to have gender balance in at least 10 occupational groups by 1993. Differences in working hours and employment rates between the genders should also be rectified, and to bring about these changes, gender equality had to be articulated with working life policy (covering fields like work environment, co-determination, working hours and employment protection). A third goal, also adopted from *Roundabout with the Ladies*, was to level out gender differences in recruitment to top posts in the public sector. A fourth goal was to address and rectify gender differences in the educational system. Equality within the family formed the fifth goal, primarily aiming for a balance between paid labour and parenthood. Here, family policy finally emerged in its own right, defined in the following way:

> Family policy aims to give all children safe and stimulating conditions
> of upbringing and to give parents the opportunity to care for and
> foster their children in the best way possible. Children have the right
> to both their parents. Both parents have the same rights to personal
> development and their own subsistence. A starting-point is that parents
> and children should have time for one another and be able to enjoy

decent standards of living. The possibility to combine parenthood with paid labour is therefore of the utmost importance. (Bill 1987/88, no. 105, p 52)

The main ingredients of family policy were reiterated – economic support to families with children, childcare, parental insurance, and public sector provision of maternity and paediatric healthcare and education. Family policy and gender equality policy were tightly integrated, for instance through the expansion of state childcare (all children over the age of one were to be covered) and the development of parental insurance (where the limited engagement of fathers was a particular challenge). To address this, childcare had to be adjusted to the demands of the labour market, but measures also had to be taken to entice men to make use of parental insurance. The way forward was improved information about how the insurance could be used within different sectors and occupational fields. The motives were twofold: it was beneficial for children to have more and improved contact with their fathers, and it would help to sustain women's position in the labour market if caring responsibilities were shared.

As gender quotas had been rejected, including the proposed sharing of parental insurance, awareness raising was the only remaining way forward for promoting gender equality policy; here the government sided with its own working group on men's roles. Another route was through research, and a study programme was established to focus on the role of men and their behaviour in society. As the number of men seeking family counselling was growing, it was hoped that research would increase understanding of the reasons behind divorce and improve the support available to men in vulnerable situations. All in all, the aim was to strengthen the role of men as fathers and parents, thereby relieving women of some of their caring obligations and enhancing their position in working life.

There was also an acknowledgement of the sometimes contradictory roles of men in families, particularly in situations of domestic violence against women. To support women in severe distress, resources for women's refuges were to be increased. Furthermore, the recently established refuges for men were to receive more support from the state.

A sixth goal concerned women's participation. The government embraced the targets set by *Roundabout with the Ladies* and pledged to increase the proportion of women in top public sector jobs from 20% to 40% between 1988 and 1995. It also made a commitment to achieve gender balance in all boards, committees and councils in the public sector within 10 years (at the end of the 1990s).

The action plan became law in 1988. It was intended to direct activities not only within central government but also among municipalities and county councils, and it was backed up by broad political consensus. While it was rather vague and general in its design, its outline became the template for family policy in the 1990s, not least its preoccupation with the role of men within the family.

Gender equality and patriarchy

> A labour market and working life policy which not only facilitates
> employment and subsistence, but also gives the chance of 'good
> work' for all people, is a cornerstone of a policy for equality between
> women and men. A social safety net that provides help and support
> during sickness (one's own or one's children's), good educational
> opportunities, and old-age security are further examples of important
> preconditions for attaining the gender-equality goals. This concerns
> basic rights, obligations and possibilities for all, irrespective of gender,
> domicile, social background or ethnic affiliation. In this sense, gender-
> equality policy and equality policy are closely coupled. (Bill 1990/91,
> no. 113, p 4)

With these words, reproducing the policy discourse that had reigned since the
late 1960s, the social democratic government summarised its gender equality
goals at the start of the 1990s (Bill 1990/91, no. 113). Just two years after the
action plan had been enacted, the government chose to evaluate its outcomes (as
well as the 1979 gender equality Act) and widen and revise the plan accordingly
(SOU 1990:41).

Some promising signs were detected; women worked virtually as much as men
and childcare had expanded dramatically and nearly doubled in size in 15 years.
The action plan had had an immediate impact on women's representation in top
positions and boards in the public sector. The number of female school principals
had increased in particular. More attention was being paid to the issue of men's
violence against women and this became one of the focal points of gender equality
policy during the decade (Wendt Höjer, 2006). In other areas, improvements were
more meagre. Women were still the primary carers in the household; moreover,
when they did work, they earned far less than men and seldom occupied the top
jobs in industry. Hence, there was a need for further reforms in gender equality
and family policy.

The newly appointed power commission provided some support and inspiration
in this endeavour, explaining why gender equality reforms had had such a limited
impact on gender equality practices (SOU 1990:44). Yvonne Hirdman, a professor
of history and feminist theoretician, developed the thesis about the primacy of
the man (the man as norm) within the framework of the commission, making
the issue of power relations central to the understanding of gender inequalities
in Sweden.

In the late 1980s, Hirdman had introduced the notion of 'genus' (as a translation
of 'gender') to explain why women have a lower value than men in society and
set about to examine the historical reasons for this (Hirdman, 1988). Women, she
argued, had been accepted within the capitalist system through their participation
in the labour market. They had also been integrated into the democratic political
system after universal suffrage was introduced in 1921. However, despite formal

equality in both the economy and the polity, women were still subordinate in society. The resistant pattern of subordination could be explained by the workings of the so-called gender system, defined as the 'structuration order of gender. This fundamental order is the precondition for other social orders' (Hirdman, 1988, p 51).

The genus system should be understood as a network of social action that creates a gender-bound pattern or logic. Both everyday life and structural features were based on two premises, the separation of women and men, and the masculine as the norm. Hirdman argued that the overriding conceptual value of the term genus system was that it highlighted how unequal social orders have been reproduced over time.

In the final report of the power commission, Hirdman wrote a section on gender equality policy, in which she argued that it had developed in such a way as to become a part of the state apparatus, which in turn had disarmed all attempts at a genuine emancipation of women:

> Since the Gender Equality Act was passed in parliament, an increasing number of formal bodies for gender-equality work have been created, and the flow of investigations and statistics has only just begun. Today, the term 'gender equality' is implanted in just about every public sphere of society and working life.... This rapidly institutionalised norm inevitably creates gender equality as an – obligatory – part of the agenda in politics and union activity, in which everything can be contained, but it has to be included.... The eager willingness with which this spirit has been created clearly shows the action-rationality of the Swedish model: to disarm and use conflicts to create new political fields, areas which no doubt receive support and enthusiasm from below. A consequence of this regulation and top-down steering is, however, that ambitions for female emancipation are formulated in terms of gender equality, which indirectly steers the strategy itself. (SOU 1990:44, pp 106-7)

Strange as it may seem, this highly critical analysis of the subordinating consequences of gender equality policy fed directly into government policy in this very field, or, in the words of the social democratic government:

> It is important to see and acknowledge that society has a long history of oppression of women. The male norm and the male superordination as a social and economic principle still live on in many, many areas. The principle has, however, been weakened and changed. It can also be said to have become more invisible with all the progress that has admittedly taken place when it comes to women's liberation. The impression that equality between women and men has already been achieved is, in fact, one of today's most important obstacles to further

development in the direction of gender equality. (Bill 1990/91, no. 113, p 7)

Hence, the government subscribed to the analysis that gender equality was about creating equal conditions, but that the male norm was still the dominant one. Gender equality work was therefore primarily concerned with conditions for women, against the backdrop of their subordination. The government put it this way: 'It is about a further shift in the power balance between the genders, in favour of women' (Bill 1990/91, no. 113, p 7).

The question – not posed for the first time, as we have seen – was how to achieve this ambitious goal. In reality, inequalities still shaped all the areas of intervention highlighted in the gender equality action plan from 1988; the gender division of labour was still in place, as was gender segregation in the educational system and in the labour market. Social insurance acted to the disadvantage of women, who worked part time to a greater extent and also took more responsibility than men for childcare. The gender wage gap remained. Men's violence against women showed no signs of decline.

To lay the foundation for a more considered approach to equality issues, economic policy had to be evaluated from a gender equality perspective. Economic policy would ideally help to achieve all the ambitious goals set out in the action plan – reduced gender segregation, a levelling of gender-based economic differences and reinforced female power within the public sector. One of the more concrete policies was the establishment of a number of professorships in gender studies in the areas of economics, political science and sociology, one of which was devoted to studies of differences in women's and men's connection to the labour market and their incomes. Other measures included vocational guidance and training programmes to rectify an uneven gender balance in some sectors, and unemployed women were encouraged to enter training programmes for occupations dominated by men. The education system also had a responsibility to redress the gender balance, for instance through information, guidance and advice to schoolchildren.

Parental insurance was also targeted. Here, it was still mainly women who participated in the scheme, a pattern that had to be changed through further awareness raising as well as through measures encouraging employers to make it easier for employees to combine parenthood and employment. Since little had so far happened in this respect, the government hinted at enforcing such measures through legislation if necessary: 'If fathers do not use the parental insurance to a much higher degree before the end of 1993, the government will consider further measures to accelerate such a development' (Bill 1990/91, no. 113, p 30). The immediate goal was, however, modest, aimed at encouraging at least two thirds of fathers to use at least some part of the parental insurance. The long-term aim was still that the responsibility for childcare should be shared between women and men. The parental insurance, which was expanded to 12 months with an income replacement element of 90%, made this ambition feasible in theory, but in reality the responsibilities were skewed and only 7% of fathers used any parental insurance in 1989 (Stanfors, 2007). Awareness raising was therefore to continue, with a particular priority to encourage men in senior positions in working life to take parental leave.

The social democratic government lost the election in 1990, and a centre-right government came into power, pledging to change Sweden from the ground up. However, continuity rather than change marked the way for gender equality policies.

Change of government and the introduction of a 'daddy month'

The centre-right government, which came into power in 1991, promised that it would do away with the social democratic heritage and give Sweden 'a new start'. As far as family policy was concerned, government opinion ranged from the cultural radicalism of the Liberal Party to the value conservatism of the Christian Democratic Party. Diversity soon led to compromise, sometimes of a rather paradoxical nature.

The government's first and only gender equality Bill was presented in 1993, entitled *Gender Equality: Shared Power – Shared Responsibilities* (Bill 1993/94, no. 147). The architect of the Bill was the Minister for Social Affairs and chairman of the Liberal Party, Bengt Westerberg. The Bill signalled continuity rather than change, and its proposals built on those presented in the action plan from 1988. Its aim was to influence the distribution of power among men and women, to ensure that 'women and men … have the same rights, obligations and possibilities in all important areas of life' (Bill 1993/94, no. 147, p 4). Even the wording signalled continuity. The centre-right government shared its predecessor's conviction that the key to success in gender equality was to solve the problems women faced in combining gainful employment and parenthood. In an attempt to improve conditions for women and men in this respect, the social services Act had been amended to establish an obligation on municipalities to offer childcare to children from the age of 12 months (Bill 1993/94, no. 147). At the same time, the new government admitted that there were problems of gender segregation in the labour market, and its remedies were by and large the same as those of the preceding social democratic government. It also continued the focus on the prevention of men's violence against women, and a commission on violence against women was appointed, which reported a few years later (SOU 1995:60).

Women's representation in industry as well as in the public sector was another area of continued political debate, and the centre-right government pressed for an increase in the number of female directors and managers in private business. Falling back on the traditional government commissions, it also appointed a women's power commission to investigate the differences in women's and men's accumulation of economic power as individuals, within families and in society at large, a subject to which we return later.

To sum up, the government described its gender equality policy goals in the following way:

- even distribution of power and influence between women and men;
- equal opportunity between men and women for economic independence
- equal conditions for women and men in enterprises and in working life, in employment and working conditions and for development within work;
- equal access to education for women and men (and girls and boys) as well as equal opportunities to develop personal ambitions, interests and talents;
- shared responsibility between women and men for childcare and household work;
- freedom from gender-related violence (Bill 1993/94, no. 147).

To achieve these goals, virtually the same as its social democratic predecessor, it was deemed necessary that a 'gender-equality perspective should be applied in all political areas. This means that proposals and decisions must be analysed from the perspective of gender equality to clarify possible consequences for women and for men, in particular within the areas of education, labour market, industrial, social and economic policy' (Bill 1993/94, no. 147, p 17).

For the first time, and in this respect the centre-right government went beyond its predecessor in its level of ambition, gender equality was supposed to permeate all political fields. However, in similar vein to other governments it referred back to the analysis of the gender system theory when grappling with the issue of continuous gender differences in society:

> Characteristic of the gender system are the principles of the separation of the genders and of men's superordination and women's subordination in different areas of society. Gender separation is illustrated by the different occupations of women and men, their respective working areas, responsibilities within the household, etc. The segregation in the labour market operates on different levels. When women have entered the labour market on a broad scale they have, to a large extent, brought with them the tasks that they previously performed in the household. These tasks have primarily been performed within the framework of the public sector. Women and men as collectives are therefore located in different sectors of the labour market, and when they are in the same sector, men tend to hold the more senior positions even when the conditions are the same. (Bill 1993/94, no. 147, pp 20-1)

Based on the analysis afforded by the power commission, the government argued that women adhered to two, often paradoxical, social imperatives – they undertake paid labour and they give birth. To manage the balance between the two, women often choose to work part time, thereby 'affirming an ideological norm which they themselves can live up to without having to engage in overly difficult negotiations with their husbands' (Bill 1993/94, no. 147, p 21). Even if individual mothers consider this a good solution, it makes women economically dependent on their partners, and, furthermore, it means that women who wish to share childcare and household responsibilities are considered to be hindering men's gainful employment. In practice, the government argued, women take responsibility for negotiating who undertakes the childcare and the housework, which leads to a gender equality serving the interests of the gender system. It is this 'unwritten gender contract' that contributes to women's main responsibility for home and children, and men's responsibility for paid labour (Bill 1993/94, no. 147, pp 21-2).

Against this background, the government proposed that gender equality policy should be directed towards the structures that reproduce unequal relations. Again, it was parental insurance that became the primary instrument in the reform agenda. At the time, women used more than 90% of the entitlement allocated to families under the parental insurance scheme. This, the government argued, meant that formal rules had not altered traditional patterns. Using the term 'the man-in-principle', meaning that men are in favour of gender equality in principle but not in their daily practice, the government believed that it could explain why men did not share caring responsibilities with women. Several factors served to explain this pattern, such as negative attitudes among employers towards male paternal leave, higher male earnings and ensuing loss of household income in cases where men take parental leave and the fact that some women 'monopolise' parental leave, seeing child-rearing as a female task. These factors notwithstanding, it was important to increase men's take-up of parental leave, the government argued, otherwise it would become practically impossible to achieve gender equality in the labour market and in the home.

A so-called Daddy Group (formally the Working Group on Fathers, Children and Working Life) had been set up by the government to enlighten and inform fathers about the importance of spending time with their children. This group succeeded the working group on men's roles of the preceding government and criticised the earlier group for its allegedly old-fashioned theoretical starting points in research on sex roles (Klinth, 2002). In its report *For the Sake of the Children* (*För barnens skull*, 1993), the new working group proposed that a 'daddy guarantee' be introduced, whereby three months of parental leave were earmarked for the father.

The government did not adopt the radical proposal of the working group, but it did propose that parental leave be allocated freely between parents with shared custody, with 30 days of leave being non-transferable. In effect, one month of parental leave was reserved for the father – the 'daddy month' in popular parlance. When the proposal was sent out for comment, most respondents were positive, with the notable exceptions of the Employers' Confederation and the Women's Organisation of the Moderate (Conservative) Party.

When the economic crisis hit Sweden, social insurance compensation levels were reduced, including those for parental insurance, although entitlement for the earmarked 'daddy month' was unaffected, in order to avoid counteracting the measures taken to encourage men to make use of parental insurance. Intense bargaining took place within the centre–right government. The Christian Democratic Party, which had opposed quotas in parental insurance, demanded that their favourite family policy reform – the cash-for-care scheme – be established as a *quid pro quo*. The cash-for-care-scheme had been implemented as a compromise in 1994, only to be abolished after six months when a new government came to power. The implementation of the cash-for-care scheme in 1994 included 2,000 Swedish kronor (about €200) per month per child between one and three years old who did not spend more than 30 hours per week in public day care. The rhetoric behind the reform called for parents to make an active choice about whether to put the children in public day care or take care of the children themselves. The critique against the reform was based on the assumption that it was probably mainly mothers who had to stay at home with their children; in other words, the reform was seen as a trap for all mothers seeking paid employment. Moreover, the reform was in itself a paradox; gender equality policy aimed to make it easier for women to enter the labour market while the cash-for-care-scheme encouraged parents (in reality, mothers) to stay at home with their children (Bergqvist, 1999).

Hence, after a decade of voluntary measures, the time seemed to be ripe for a more radical reform of parental insurance – awareness raising had proved to be insufficient to change men's attitudes, and legislation was deemed necessary to alter the patterns of responsibility within Swedish families. In addition, the government proposed and enacted major changes in the gender equality Act; it is here that we find the first major ideological breaks with the gender equality policy legacy.[1] While the social democratic governments had primarily relied on the labour market parties to regulate workplace matters (including those of gender equality), the centre–right government established the principle that the gender equality Act prevailed over voluntary agreements. This was a contested stance, as it intervened in one of the most conflictual periods in the Swedish labour market, when the position of trade unions had already been weakened with the advent of mass unemployment; it was widely interpreted as yet another blow against the inclusion of the labour market parties in public policy making. It also pitted gender equality against the principle of self-determination in the labour market, splitting the previously close integration between labour market regulation and gender equality policy.

The women's power commission

The women's power commission was appointed in 1994 by the centre–right government to investigate the differences in women's and men's supply of economic power as individuals, within families and in society at large. The commission was given renewed confidence by the social democratic government and reported most of its findings in 1998.

The commission was set up to investigate the gendered distribution of economic power and resources. It was not a traditional government commission working with a defined political reform in mind, but rather a research project working for the government. It reported its work in the form of 13 lengthy studies covering three broad themes: family, working life/labour market and welfare policies. Even its final report read more like a research report (or rather a summary of the previous reports) than an ordinary government commission report (SOU 1998:6).

The 13 reports presented state-of-the-art research on the three themes, both for feminist empirical investigations and for theoretical elaborations. The reports showed that women's studies had expanded and become more heterogeneous. The individual reports covered a wide range of issues, including management recruitment, economic power, labour market positions, social insurance, wage development, trade union policy, the division of labour in the household, historical perspectives on the 'women's issue' and so on.

The final report synthesised all of these findings, pointing out in its conclusion that Sweden had been named by the UN as the most gender-equal country in the world in 1995. If Sweden were deemed good enough, the report contended, it could only be because the situation was even worse in other countries. Sweden, it concluded, was not an equal or gender-equal country. On the contrary, argued the commission, the reports clearly showed that 'gender-equal Sweden' was a myth. The labour market was still segregated, and family life was very much marked by unequal relations between women and men. Men still earned more money, had better and more qualified (full-time) jobs and used parental leave to a lesser degree than women. Women worked part time and earned less than men, and their careers suffered, not least because they were more likely than men to take care of children, the home and older parents. The commission also exposed the myth of the rational, efficient working life in Sweden; how could it be efficient, it asked, when power relations between women and men were so skewed?

Even though the commission's report was primarily analytical rather than prescriptive, it made some practical suggestions. For example, it wanted to introduce an agency under the auspices of the labour market parties to facilitate a gender-neutral wage structure. A somewhat original proposal was to initiate yet another commission, this time on Work, Life and Welfare for All (Arbete, Liv och Välfärd för Alla, known as ALVA after Alva Myrdal). It was envisaged that it would operate with a more practical and concrete mandate, and make suggestions that would radically transform unequal relations in households and in the labour market, with the visionary aim of outlining 'a society in which there is a balance between on the one hand the demands and possibilities of production, and on the other hand the welfare and quality of life of individuals' (SOU 1998:6, p 6).

While the commission's recommendation fell on deaf ears, its many reports contributed to shaping the gender-policy agenda of the coming decade. At the same time, gender equality policy continued its radicalisation.

Gender mainstreaming and the gender power order: new concepts and old problems

Gender equality policy was reinforced with a number of new concepts during the 1990s. The gender system was one of them. In the mid-1990s, two additional concepts came to influence and further shape the discourse and social practice of gender equality policy – gender mainstreaming and the gender power order.

Gender mainstreaming as a concept had already been introduced in 1985 at the United Nations (UN) Third World Conference on Women in Nairobi, then connected to political empowerment of women in the third world. In 1995, the UN held its Fourth World Conference on Women, in Beijing. At the conference, an action plan on gender equality was ratified by a majority of the member countries, which included a pledge to integrate gender equality in all issues and decisions taken by the governments. One of the strategies advocated was 'gender mainstreaming'.

The official UN definition of gender mainstreaming was outlined as

> a globally accepted strategy for promoting gender equality. Mainstreaming is not an end in itself but a strategy, an approach, a means to achieve the goal of gender equality. Mainstreaming involves ensuring that gender perspectives and attention to the goal of gender equality are central to all activities – policy development, research, advocacy/dialogue, legislation, resource allocation, and planning, implementation and monitoring of programmes and projects. (www.un.org/womenwatch/osagi/gendermainstreaming.htm)

Thus, the concept moved from being connected to empowerment in the third world to becoming a worldwide political strategy. The European Union (EU) had also commenced its work on gender mainstreaming, and Sweden – an EU member since 1995 – took an active part in the EU Gender Equality Committee. During 1995 and 1996, the committee primarily addressed issues pertaining to the UN conference, primarily to ensure that a gender equality perspective was integrated in all areas of EU activity and engagement.

A similar process of gender mainstreaming – from nebulous concept to social practice – took place in Sweden, where the Liberal Minister for Gender Equality, Bengt Westerberg, introduced the idea in 1994 (just before losing power to the social democrats, who returned to power the same year with Ingvar Carlsson and later Göran Persson as prime minister). In its first policy declaration, the newly elected government pledged to let gender equality permeate all its activities. Gender equality was no longer to be a residual policy, operating in isolation from other policy areas, but rather a natural part of all political activity. In a memorandum from 1996 on gender equality, gender mainstreaming was, for the first time, taken up in government discourse:

[Gender mainstreaming] has been highlighted in international work for gender equality. Mainstreaming can be translated into the incorporation of a gender-equality perspective within the mainstream of every policy field. Issues of gender equality cannot be treated individually or apart from ordinary activities. A gender-equality perspective is an obvious part of all work. The English term [gender mainstreaming] is used to stress that it is not just a matter of compensating for the shortcomings of one of the genders or to integrate women's issues in structures that have been developed on the basis of male norms. It is instead about a brand new point of view. And new ones developed on the basis of analyses of the different conditions that apply to women and men. (Skr.1996/97:41)

Gender mainstreaming as a strategy has been debated since its first day in politics. One question revolves around whether gender mainstreaming contributes to a real transformation in gender relations as its proponents argue, or if, as the critics maintain, it has been reduced to mere methods and techniques (Daly, 2005). Another contested issue is the actual policy environment in which gender mainstreaming should be incorporated; in many countries, gender equality is often contested and its impact reduced (Walby, 2005). This dilemma is also related to a potential conflict between the relationship between women and men 'because of unequal power relations and cooperation between the sexes presumed by gender mainstreaming' (Sainsbury and Bergqvist, 2009, p 217). Finally, many feminists contend that gender mainstreaming is an elite project, which in many cases excludes women working in, for example, women's movements (Verloo, 2007).

Political scientists Diane Sainsbury and Christina Bergqvist (2009) have analysed gender mainstreaming in Sweden. They argue that Sweden is noteworthy in that gender equality has been an important political strategy since the 1970s, which means that 'the introduction of gender mainstreaming was superimposed on a specific type of gender policy regime that has had gender equality as its principal aim' (Sainsbury and Bergqvist, 2009, p 218). The first gender mainstreaming measure introduced in Sweden was the introduction of gender training for cabinet members and other senior officials and administrators in government ministries and agencies in the early 2000s. The incorporation of gender equality into inquiry commissions mainly in terms of training and education was especially important given their key role in the policy-making process (Sainsbury and Bergqvist, 2009, p 221). Gender mainstreaming thus became the central strategy for maintaining gender equality.

In 2001, a government working group evaluated the work on gender mainstreaming that had begun in 1994. In its evaluation report, the group argued that many senior officials were not sufficiently committed to the project and that the strategy did not have any impact on working practices. Moreover, the report pointed out that the implementation of gender mainstreaming often depended on a single individual, mainly someone who already worked in the area of equal opportunities. Sainsbury and Bergqvist summarised the evaluation as follows: 'Despite its general enthusiasm for gender mainstreaming, the working group's report was characterized by a strong critical undertone and an awareness of the problems of implementing a gender mainstreaming strategy' (Sainsbury and Bergqvist, 2009, p 223). The evaluation sparked off an intense debate on the practice of gender mainstreaming. One of the major results was the construction of a national action plan for gender equality under the auspices of a central administrative agency for gender equality (also suggested in the 2006 Bill on gender equality). While the Bill was approved in 2006, the proposals were scrapped when the social democrats lost the election in 2006. Instead, the centre-right government established a new ministry for integration and gender equality, investigated further in Chapter Six.

It was not only the concept of gender mainstreaming that occurred within gender-equal policy discourse (and to some extent also policy practice). Other changes in the language of gender equality policy were also under way. As we have seen, the concept of a 'gender system' had been adopted in the policy discourse by the early 1990s. In the-mid 1990s, a new term from feminist studies entered the policy vocabulary as a means to understand the mechanisms behind inequality – the gender power order:

> Power and influence are distributed unevenly between women and men, in society and within families. A major part of the structures of society is developed on the basis of a male norm. This norm, which is visible and invisible, is a major influence on how women and men organise their family life. This is often referred to as the gender-power order in modern women's studies, referring to men's relative superordination and women's relative subordination, and it is still maintained and reproduced in our society. It is done consciously or unconsciously, through decisions and actions in everyday life, in working life, in politics and in the private sector. These decisions and actions tend to give women worse conditions than those of men in most areas. Changing this order is the most important challenge for gender-equality policy. (Skr. 1996/97:41)

The gender power order as a concept illustrates the upcoming radicalisation of gender equality policy; by the end of the 1990s and the beginning of the 2000s, radical feminism came to dominate gender equality policies and the biggest party in Sweden, the Social Democratic Party, proclaimed itself to be a feminist party. This is examined further in Chapter Six.

Conclusion

Rethinking gender equality policy in the age of neoliberalism

After 1980, the era of significant reform in Swedish politics was over. Financial constraints and ideological changes of direction abruptly halted the seemingly endless expansion of welfare. Other elements of the post-war compact also came under fire; corporatist interest mediation and expert-led government commissions, for example, were both deemed unnecessary and counterproductive in the new political climate. This was just the beginning of the transformation of the Swedish model, however. The economic crisis of the 1990s resulted in the dismantling of the Swedish model, with mass unemployment and cutbacks in social services and social insurance schemes. Reflecting the (alleged) accelerating individualisation process, the family entity was more or less abandoned in policy discourse and was replaced by a focus on the experiences of individual women and men. These changes shaped family policy developments between 1980 and the late 1990s.

The re-evaluation of family policy had already begun in the early 1980s, when two critical evaluations of the family and gender equality policies pursued in the 1970s emerged. The main critics of gender equality policies were feminists who challenged dominant beliefs about gender equality, caring responsibilities and men's roles in the family. The gender neutrality discourse had, they argued, masked actual differences between women and men, and these differences once again came to the fore in policy debates. The emerging field of masculinity studies also shaped the renegotiation of family policy ambition and direction. Masculinity studies made men's shortcomings as fathers and carers abundantly clear. Their lack of engagement made them as a group responsible for women's subordinated position in the labour market, and men's family practices undermined the noble goals of gender equality policy. A new family paradox emerged: women were still the caring heads of the family, limiting their working life connections despite gender equality law and gender-neutral reforms.

The massive critique of gender equality policy – stressing the impossibility of achieving gender equality without transforming gender relations in the family – was to a certain extent accepted and adopted by politicians. The introduction of the concept of gender system (referring to a thesis about the 'structuration order of gender', and the primacy of men as a norm) was an attempt to reshape and revitalise family policy. The perspective was clearly informed by a structural account of power relations, arguing that women were structurally subordinated to men; even if policy instruments like gender-neutral parental insurance or an individualised taxation system empowered women, they only did so in theory as they were undermined by family practices and the hierarchically structured roles of women and men. Gender equality policy, reflecting the perspective, consequently emphasised the importance of changing power relations 'in favour of women'. Gender equality policy was therefore (as in earlier family policy making), geared towards women, after an interlude of gender neutrality, only this time with a different aim.

This transformation of the grounds for gender equality policy coincided with the rise of neoliberalism in Sweden, despite the country's considerable social democratic legacy. Such a circumscribed neoliberalism (as David Harvey coined it) shaped family policy in two paradoxical ways: one that focused on defamiliarisation and individualisation in the social insurance system and another where the structural subordination of women informed policy activism. The resulting incoherence between defamiliarisation and structural explanations of female subordination represented a fundamental family policy paradox in the period.

The gendered division of care work

The concept of care was central in the gender equality debates of the period; gender equality would only be achieved, the argument went, if responsibility for care work were shared between women and men. The question that remained was *how* shared responsibilities could ever be realised.

To begin with, men were seen as being responsible for inequality within families as well as for women's subordination in the labour market. The impact of gender-neutral policy was critically scrutinised, and it seemed obvious that decades of gender equality rhetoric on shared parenthood had failed utterly. Parenthood was still a female domain, and not a role shared by mothers and fathers.

To reduce the pressure on women and to foster new roles and responsibilities within the family, the government established 'men's groups' to explore men's resistance to caring responsibilities and to introduce men to gender-equal thinking. These ambitions culminated in the emergence of 'daddy politics', which in turn coincided with the rise of a gender-equal policy aiming to increase the number of senior women in public sector jobs, achieve equal gender representation in government and combat violence against women, that is, a politics 'in favour of women'.

Men's participation in care work was indeed a priority for the new 'daddy politics' and it was embraced by (almost) all political parties. The centre-right government (1991-94) went even further than its predecessor and introduced a 'daddy month' in parental insurance, where one month of entitlement was reserved for fathers in a bid to encourage men to take on the role of childcare.

While a new hegemony seemed to have emerged, there was no shortage of policy paradoxes, as evidenced by another family policy reform, the cash-for-care system. The reform was the result of a compromise to appease the Christian Democratic Party, which had opposed the quota system in the parental insurance system. While family policy aimed to make it easier for women to join the labour market, the cash-for-care scheme encouraged mothers to stay at home with their children. Hence, one reform nullified another, with some policies aimed at transgressing traditional gender roles and others at preserving them.

By the mid-1990s, a new concept entered the gender policy vocabulary in Sweden – gender mainstreaming. Originally introduced by the UN, it came to imply that a gender equality perspective should be incorporated in all policy fields. Gender mainstreaming thus became the dominant strategy for gender equality policy, focusing on administrative practices rather than gender roles within the family. These were instead taken up by another concept – that of the gender power order – introduced and incorporated into gender equality policy discourse at the end of the 1990s. This concept focused on a power-based analysis of gender relations and marked the beginning of the radicalisation of gender equality policy in the new millennium.

Note

[1] A core principle in Swedish labour market regulation had been the devolution of power to the labour market parties through collective bargaining. The reformed gender equality Act resulted in the government intervening more directly in labour market regulation, thereby bypassing voluntary agreements between the labour market parties (Bill 1990/91, no. 113).

SIX

Family policy and gender equality in the new millennium

The first decade of the new millennium has been a dramatic period in the history of gender equality and family policy. Starting with an analysis of how (radical) feminism came to the fore in the policy battles of election campaigns in the early 2000s, which resulted in the establishment of a new political party called Feminist Initiative, this chapter explores how the Swedish political landscape turned feminist. However, the initial success of feminist policy ambitions was to end in conflict and the resulting political death of feminism. Meanwhile, family policy developed, built on the foundations laid in earlier decades; the expansion of the parental insurance scheme and the introduction of a maximum fee for public day care were the main developments before the change of government in 2006. Two exceptions to this established pattern were the introduction of much longed-for legislation in 2002 on the right of same-sex couples to adopt children, and, in 2005, on the right of lesbian couples to use reproduction technologies (insemination) in public medical centres.

The need for feminism in policy making was not the only debate among policymakers and intellectuals. Another, closely related, discussion became more prominent during the first years of the new millennium, namely the debate on gender equality and diversity. Post-colonial researchers argued that the high-profile gender equality policies in Sweden paradoxically did not acknowledge different experiences among women (and men) and questioned the very idea of women-friendliness. This resulted in a heated debate on 'Swedishness' and structural racism.

As discussed later, the period 2000-10 has been marked by general political turbulence. Following the quick and unexpectedly strong recovery of the Swedish economy in 1999 and 2000, with growth rates of around 4% and a dramatic decrease in unemployment, the tone of the economic, social and labour market policy debate changed. Throughout the 2000s, the economy had been relatively strong, even though the end of the dotcom boom, which accounted for much of the economic upswing around the turn of the millennium, hit Sweden hard. Indeed, Sweden, like most other high-income countries, enjoyed a period of uninterrupted economic growth between 2003 and 2008, and, although not immune to the current world economic crisis, Sweden has not been as badly affected as many other nations within the European Union (Schön, 2010).

Despite these relatively positive developments in the economy, unemployment (especially among migrants) and high levels of sick leave (especially among women and older workers) continued to plague the social democratic government, and these formed two of the key campaigning issues for the centre-right opposition. In the 2006 election, the opposition parties, now joined together to form the 'alliance parties', were able to capitalise on the issue of 'labour market marginalisation' (*utanförskap*) and presented several radical reforms of labour market policy, with implications for both gender equality and family policy. These reforms included the so-called gender equality bonus as well as the reintroduction of the cash-for-care-scheme. Moreover, as well as making individual freedom of choice one of their main points of departure, the alliance parties acknowledged gender inequalities, which led to the introduction of family policy reforms aimed at making it easier for women to enter the labour market. Thus, two family policy paradoxes emerged at the end of the first decade of the new millennium: first was the introduction of the cash-for-care-scheme, which was counterintuitive to the idea of full employment for all citizens, and second was the ambition to create freedom of choice for those individuals being steered into the labour market by family policy and gender equality policy reforms .This will be further investigated in the last section of this chapter.

Feminist Initiative and radical feminism

During the election campaign of 1998, questions about women's position in society arose in the policy discourse, introduced mainly by Gudrun Schyman, chairperson of the Left Party. Although gender equality policy remained a priority, the election campaign rarely dealt with issues of gender and family. Schyman argued for a better and more effective gender equality policy agenda, aimed at improving the circumstances of poorer women and single mothers. These were the groups badly hit by cuts in the public sector caused by the economic crisis, and as a result the Left Party got 12% of the votes and became the third biggest party in Sweden. The gender equality rhetoric turned out to be a political success. The same year, the Centre Party, the Liberal Party and the Green Party proclaimed themselves to be feminist parties. By 2000, Prime Minister Göran Persson claimed to be feminist, as did the social democratic government in 2001. By this time, the Moderate Party had also cultivated a 'bourgeois feminist' profile. However, although all political parties were feminists in rhetoric and discourse, no real change (for example, in the level of salaries for low-paid women) occurred. This situation caused frustration among voters and above all among many feminist campaigners.

Gudrun Schyman left the Left Party at the end of 2003 and began lobbying for feminist adult education. She gained the support of the Minister for Gender Equality, Margareta Winberg. In April 2005, she was one of the founders of the establishment of a new political party, Feminist Initiative (F!). F! quickly became popular, especially among other well-known feminists in universities and on the cultural scene. The establishment of F! almost immediately become a threat to the other political parties. The Social Democratic Party secretary, Marita Ulvskog, launched a feminist network (operating alongside the Social Democratic Women's Organisation) called Feministas. Most of the other parties claimed that gender equality was one of the most important questions of modern time and it was to become the key issue in the upcoming election of 2006.

However, F! was plagued by internal conflicts over the alleged heteronormativity of some of its leading figures, conflicts that increasingly became the subject of ridicule in the media. This negative coverage included a television documentary on radical feminism in the autumn of 2005 that scrutinised the national organisation for women's refuges (Roks) and its impact on gender equality policy. Roks was portrayed as an extremist organisation that based its activities (and political lobbying) on theories of male evil within satanist networks and had questionable influence over senior figures in gender equality policy making. The programme targeted two women, Eva Lundgren, a professor of sociology at Uppsala University, and Margareta Winberg. Winberg in particular was portrayed as a militant ally with skewed feminist theoreticians, one-sidedly emphasising women's structural subordination to men in the government's attempts to comprehend and address remaining inequalities in Swedish society.

The documentary triggered a lively and sometimes fierce debate on the influence of radical feminism on gender equality policy. While the programme attracted much criticism, and was berated by the Swedish Broadcasting Commission for its partiality, the journalist behind the documentary, Evin Rubar, was awarded Swedish Television's gender equality prize and received the national prize for investigative journalism. Meanwhile, there were serious consequences for those portrayed in the programme. The vice-chancellor of Uppsala University appointed a team to scrutinise Eva Lundgren's research, and it concluded that Lundgren could not be accused of falsification. The chairperson of Roks resigned, and a third of Roks' member centres left the organisation. The impact was also felt further afield; F! disappeared from the political scene and the strong political focus on feminism and gender inequalities – the wave on which F! had been riding – more or less died out.

The waning of feminism's influence over the political landscape does not, however, imply that issues relating to inequality or unequal relations between women and men vanished. On the contrary, mainstream gender equality (or state feminism) was still very much alive, as illustrated in a government commission report from 2005 that, among other things, suggested the introduction of a new administration/authority of gender equality (analysed further later). Hence, gender mainstreaming still existed but separated from the progressive feminist movement.

> It was highly controversial when F! argued that men have to abandon
> their privileges. Not least in a country like Sweden, where gender
> equality policy rests on a silent agreement on implying a win-win
> situation. It is a paradox, since all gender equality policy is about
> redistribution of power and resource, from men to women. But it
> can't be said in the open, and F! challenged this understanding. (Drude
> Dahlerup, professor of political science at Stockholm University in
> the magazine *Focus*, 31 March 2006)

Feminism within the policy discourse, then, was dead, but not before the government and many other political parties turned feminist. But what did a feminist government really mean?

A feminist government?

The social democrats won the 2002 election by a narrow margin. This time, the gender equality programme was devised in collaboration with the social democrats' allies, the Green Party and the Left Party. The rhetoric was familiar:

> Our society is still characterised by a gender-power order, despite a long history of work for gender equality. This work must be given a more feminist orientation in the future. This means that we must be aware of the existence of a gender-power order where women are subordinate and men superior, and have the will to change it. This also implies that the government views male and female as 'social constructions', that is, gender patterns that are created on the basis of upbringing, culture, economic frameworks, power structures and political ideology. Gender patterns are created and maintained both at the personal level and on a societal level. This structure has not been changed despite that fact that the representation of women and men in some areas of society is beginning to converge in quantitative terms. If we do not break today's gender-power order, we will not achieve an equal society. (Skr. 2002/03: 140, p 5)

The novelty in the discourse was the notion that gender equality work should become 'feminist'. 'Feminist' in this respect was highly specific and referred to a mixture of the notion of the gender power order and theories about men's violence against women. This theoretical mixture thus became the basis for the government's discourse and policy deliberations. Adhering to the standards of the 'gender power order', gender equality policy was again labelled a grandiose failure, unable to alter the structures that underpinned unequal power relations between women and men. Even though political reforms had been devised to alter gender relations, they met with stubborn resistance rooted in the norms and values that pervaded predominant views of caring responsibilities and educational choices: 'The political reforms are met by a gender system which can reproduce and reinforce notions of fundamental differences between women and men' (Skr. 2002/03: 140, p 8)

The government also warned against over-optimistic accounts based on quantitative indicators of gender equality. By focusing only on representation within senior positions, or the gender balance in the labour market in general, one risked disregarding the importance of power. The new mandate for gender equality policy therefore had to be to address power differences between women and men, by making the gender power order visible and by attacking its underpinning structures (Skr. 2002/03: 140, p 5).

The way forward was fivefold: continuing the work for equal representation and an even distribution of power and influence; enforcing the principle of equal pay for equal work; combating men's violence against women, as well as prostitution and sex trafficking; enhancing men's engagement in gender equality; and counteracting the sexualisation of public space.

Awareness raising and other measures to change attitudes (through campaigns, projects and so on) were to be coordinated to improve their impact. Gender mainstreaming was to be expanded through the integration of a 'gender perspective' into all public sector activities. All such activities were to be subjected to an analysis of their consequences on gender relations. Gender equality was also to inform integration policy, although there were many difficulties with this, not least when it came to honour-related violence. In the short term, potential victims of honour-related violence were to be offered sheltered housing (Skr. 2002/03:140, p 32). Recently arrived migrants were to be educated in the 'Swedish' approach to gender equality, an approach, it was argued, that could be taught to 'ignorant' new arrivals. In doing so, cases of honour-related violence were expected to dwindle and the norms of gender equality to spread and become generalised within Swedish society. We return to the consequences of this policy later.

Minister for Gender Equality, Margareta Winberg, discussed earlier in relation to her support of Gudrun Schyman's initiatives to feminist adult education, and of feminist research and researchers, also openly stated that she would apply the gender power theory in her work. This made her highly controversial and the subject of much public debate and criticism.

Although dispute and controversy characterised the gender equality debates of the early 2000s, a number of significant reforms were enacted. Two of the most significant were the introduction of maximum charges for childcare and another month of parental insurance earmarked for the father.

Family policy reforms in the new millennium

In 2001, the social democratic government honoured its election promise of a maximum charge for childcare as part of an overhaul of childcare provision and organisation. Until then, municipalities had been free to set their own childcare fees and make their own rules about eligibility for childcare for unemployed parents and students with children. In 2001, the rules governing childcare fees were changed, with the aim of increasing the provision of childcare, improving the economic circumstances of families with children and supporting dual-income couples. The most important element in the reform package was the maximum fee for childcare, which put a ceiling on childcare costs, both in relative terms (as a percentage of parents' incomes) and in absolute terms (with a maximum fee) (Bill 1999/2000, no. 129). All municipalities had to offer parents who were unemployed or claiming parental insurance at least 15 hours of childcare per week. Pre-schools for all children aged four and five were also established, and all municipalities were obliged to offer childcare places to children over the age of one.

With municipalities enjoying widespread autonomy in Sweden, the system of maximum fees for childcare was voluntary. However, those municipalities that joined the scheme received compensation from the state for the reduced fees paid by parents. By 2003, all municipalities were covered by the system. The main motive behind the reform was to increase the supply of labour, encouraging parents who did not work to do so and those who already had a job to increase their working hours (Lundin et al, 2007, p 3). The social democrats also wanted to make it easier for women to enter the labour market and wanted to promote the interests of the female supporters of Gudrun Schyman and the Left Party.

The economic impact on families with children was dramatic, as childcare costs were halved overnight. Childcare provision increased, and by 2004, 92% of all children aged three to six took part in state-funded childcare. The impact on labour supply was less clear-cut. An analysis of the years 2001 and 2003 shows that the impact was limited at the time, although one clear trend was for men with an academic degree to work longer hours after the reform (Lundin et al, 2007). Childcare provision was also closely connected to the parental insurance scheme.

Parental insurance was again the subject of public investigations in the 2000s. In 2002, the insurance was prolonged (to 390 days), and the earmarking was expanded to two months for each of the parents, with the explicit aim of 'further improving the possibilities of parents to combine family and work' (Bill 2000/01, no. 44, p 1). In 2005, a government commission proposed a more thorough reform of the insurance, suggesting an increase in the earmarked parts of the insurance in order to 'in the long term contribute to genuinely equal parenthood and a more gender-equal labour market' (SOU 2005:73, p 18). This was yet another, albeit unsuccessful, attempt to alter the uneven distribution of parental insurance.

In 2004, 19% of parental insurance days, and a third of the days available under the insurance scheme for sick children, went to fathers. However, it was not only a matter of the number of days available, but also of how families made use of their entitlement: women tended to take time off in an uninterrupted stretch, whereas men took shorter, more frequent, spells of leave (SOU 2005:66).

The commission report was highly critical of how the parental insurance scheme was reported in official statistics, which, it argued, obscured the intricacies of how parents used it. The commission was therefore also sceptical about the long-term impact of its own proposal, namely the individualisation of parental insurance: 'women's absence from the labour market would probably still be longer' (SOU 2005:66, p 260). This dilemma highlighted issues of class and parenthood, something that was further developed in an LO report that argued that the way in which parental insurance was distributed among men and women was related to class. It claimed that distribution patterns were more uneven in low-income than in high-income families, and one explanation put forward for this was that women on low incomes, with a weaker connection to the labour market and more repetitive work, actually preferred to make maximum use of the parental insurance. Another study, conducted by the Ministry of Finance, concluded that women with a weak position in the labour market lacked the incentive to influence their husbands to take parental leave (Jansson et al, 2003). What these studies have in common is a focus on how the distribution of parental insurance is shaped by women's conditions in the labour market. The distribution of parental insurance reflected the variations in women's position in the labour market, even though women in general, irrespective of whether they had children or whether they shared the parental insurance with their partners, were in a weaker position (SOU 2005:66, p 262). The outlook for gender equality in the labour market was certainly gloomy, and it seemed as if all instruments at the disposal of gender equality policy were more or less powerless.

The suggestion to individualise parental insurance was not implemented. The issue was too controversial among the established parties and there is still no consensus within the Social Democratic, Green and the Left Parties, nor among the centre-right parties. And just as in the reports discussed earlier, the disagreements are about issues relating to class, income and gender.

Gay, lesbian and bisexual parenthood

One of the issues closely related to the use of the parental insurance system concerns eligibility and the qualifications necessary to become a parent. The nuclear family – and in particular women – has served as a starting point for virtually all family policy reforms. Other groups have slowly been incorporated, but while both fathers and single mothers have been acknowledged in family policy discourse and practice since the 1960s, homosexual families have received little attention.

Before 1944, homosexuality and homosexual relations were illegal in Sweden and termed a 'crime against nature' (*brott som mot naturen är*). Although a criminal code of this name did not mention the word homosexuality, it was generally accepted by lawyers that it referred to homosexual relations (Edenheim, 2005, p 27). In the 1930s, the issue was taken up by the social democrats and debated in political circles. In 1941, a government commission report suggested abolishing the code. It was eventually abolished in 1944 and thereafter legal debates on homosexuality focused solely on age limits for homosexual relations (Edenheim, 2005; see also Rydström, 2001).

In the 1970s, parliament concluded that 'homosexuality was an acceptable form of lifestyle', and as a result homosexuality was no longer seen as a psychiatric disease. A commission was appointed to investigate social conditions for homosexuals and explore the possibilities of introducing a law for cohabiting homosexuals (which should correlate to the law for heterosexual couples). The law was implemented in 1988 (Edenheim, 2005).

The number of government commission reports relating to homosexuality increased between 1980 and 2000. A considerable change in the composition of the commissions was obvious, from the dominance of medical experts to increasing numbers of social scientists representing the experts. This led to a shift in the discourse on homosexuality, which resulted in a debate at the beginning of the 1990s on the legal status of cohabiting homosexuals and the introduction of a law on registered partnership in 1994.[1] In 1999, an ombudsman for homosexuality was introduced, and in the same year, the social democratic government summoned a commission to analyse the everyday life of children in homosexual families, and to investigate whether there were any differences between homosexual and heterosexual couples in terms of their rights and opportunities to adopt children. If the commission concluded that there were legal differences that should be removed, they should also consider whether lesbians should be granted access to reproduction technologies, such as donor insemination.

The commission report (SOU 2001:10) was an in-depth investigation on existing research in the field and also contained the results of a study carried out by the commission itself on the conditions among children in homosexual families. The commission found that there were no differences in conditions between children in homosexual and heterosexual families (in terms of psychological development, well-being in the family and the surrounding society, levels of care and so on), leading the commission to suggest that homosexual registered couples should be given the same opportunities to adopt children as heterosexual married couples. Moreover, the commission suggested that registered partners should be able to adopt the other partner's child, as in the case of married heterosexual couples.

Another issue raised in the commission's report was the right of lesbians to donor insemination. The law only allowed this for married women, which had forced Swedish lesbians to go abroad to undergo donor insemination. The commission suggested, in line with its other proposals, that cohabiting lesbian couples or those living in registered partnerships should have access to the same reproduction technologies (insemination) as heterosexual married or cohabiting couples (SOU 2001:10). In 2005, the right of lesbian couples to donor insemination was introduced and the pregnant woman's partner was legally considered a parent.

The development of rights for homosexual families has always been marked by normative assumptions, with the heterosexual nuclear family ideal as the starting point. Historian Sara Edenheim's critical examination of government commissions on homosexuality from the 1930s onwards shows that they were on shaky ground to begin with: 'Those who are constructed as sexual deviants are ascribed various wishes and needs that all depart from the monogamous, heterosexual nuclear family as a role model' (Edenheim, 2005, p 193). Edenheim's analysis also shows that investigations of children in homosexual and heterosexual families have always used the heterosexual family as a prototype for homosexuals and have assumed that homosexual couples must perform better than heterosexual parents to be accepted as 'good parents'; homosexuality becomes an exception from the heterosexual family ideal in family policy debates and suggestions. Equality between, and equal treatment of, homosexuality and heterosexuality has thus not yet been realised in Swedish public discourse or policy making.

Gender equality policy and diversity

In the 1990s and the beginning of the 2000s, questions relating to the concept and practical use of gender equality entered the policy landscape. The debate on immigration led to the broadening of the whole concept of equality, from its orientation towards gender equality to a focus on universal rights irrespective of ethnic background, sexual orientation or disability. This was not a painless transition, however, and it posed considerable challenges to both researchers (primarily of feminist and post-colonial orientation) and politicians. Several issues surfaced: Which measures are the most efficient? Should affirmative action or more evolutionary and voluntary processes reign? Are migrants confronted with discrimination based on (alleged) cultural differences, or does Swedish society reshape discrimination on a structural and racist basis?

As we have seen, the social democratic government presented a gender equality strategy for the 21st century. The goals of gender mainstreaming and the inclusion of a gender equality perspective throughout the political landscape were emphasised – as was the conclusion that the set goals had not been attained. The report *Gender Equality Policy on the Eve of the 21st Century* (Skr. 1999/2000:2) was the subject of many of the theoretical and empirical discussions of the women's power commission, as were studies of men's violence against women. The goal of gender equality policy was summarised in the report as 'a fair distribution of economic and political power'. Once again, the government pinpointed the gender power order as the key obstacle to genuine gender equality: 'It is about breaking the social structure which is still ruling and which tells us every day that men are the norm and women the exception, men are superior and women subordinate, men have great power, women little' (Skr. 1999/2000:2, p 2).

Nonetheless, the report was characterised by a certain degree of complacency. The Minister for Gender Equality, Margareta Winberg, argued that Sweden had come a long way, 'yes indeed, farthest in the world' (Skr. 1999/2000:2, p 6). She also offered to share the Swedish experience, 'our Swedish model of gender equality', with the rest of the world (Skr. 1999/2000:2, p 6). A few years later, in the wake of a tragic murder of a young woman originating from Kurdistan, the Minister of Integration, Mona Sahlin, argued that 'we have to find ways to force immigrant men to accept Swedish values such as freedom and gender equality' (DN 010608, cited in Carbin, 2008, p 29). The Integration Board followed this up by introducing the idea of teaching migrant boys and men how to understand Swedish values such as gender equality. In this context, migrant families were constructed as patriarchal and hierarchal and 'the Swedish family was ... said to be non-hierarchical and it was declared that every individual represents herself before Swedish law' (Carbin, 2008, p 31).

Statements such as these created a rather heated debate, when their ideological foundations – where Sweden was constructed as a model country, where gender equality was deep-seated and formed a natural part of the national culture (to be exported to the rest of the world) – were scrutinised by feminist and post-colonial researchers. These critics argued that Swedish authorities had constructed a division between those adhering to 'Swedish gender equality thinking' and others, primarily migrants from other parts of the world, who were seen as ignorant of the virtues of equality thinking (de los Reyes et al, 2002). Post-colonial feminists thereby argued that Sweden was a part of the colonial heritage and that a colonial mentality shows in policy making, found in the concept of culture; in order to create a Swedish identity, culture has, since the 1970s, been used to contrast Swedish culture from 'the Other' (mainly migrants from outside Europe) (de los Reyes et al, 2002). Culture therefore became a tool among politicians to describe and explain socioeconomic differences between the majority and minorities, where cultural differences form the very basis for the development of integration policy (Ålund, 2000). In this context, the meanings and understandings of diversity (*mångfald*) never included the idea of a melting pot, where different cultural backgrounds shape new social conditions, but were based rather on the integration of 'other' cultures into the imagined Swedish culture.

This became obvious when so-called 'honour-related violence' became the subject of heated debate at the beginning of the 2000s. Politicians argued that this could only be halted if men who accepted this type of violence on cultural grounds learned to respect Swedish gender equality ideals. The fact that some 'Swedish' men are violent against 'Swedish' women was addressed in structural rather than cultural terms, as in this context women as a group were seen as subordinate to men. Hence, different templates guided different analyses of men's violence, one for 'immigrant' men and another for 'Swedish' men (Carbin, 2008).

In the wake of the debate on 'honour-related violence' and increasing discussions on discrimination against migrants, a government commission on structural discrimination concluded that the discrimination was connected to integration policies and it even suggested that the Integration Board should be closed down. It also suggested that the distinction between migrant men and ethnic Swedes in relation to violence must come to an end (SOU 2005:56; SOU 2006:79).

As mentioned in Chapter One, many post-colonial feminists have argued that the political culture and debate in Sweden are shaped by a deep-seated notion of Swedishness, where the gender equality ideal and gender equality policy figure prominently. This notion is accompanied by great difficulties in integrating gender equality policy with diversity politics:

> Nordic state feminist responses to the challenges of diversity are likely to be particularly anxious given that gender equality has such a privileged status in these countries and has not generally been attentive to differences among women, frequently obscuring the experiences of immigrant and ethnic women. (Squires, 2007, p 161)

Diversity has therefore not emerged as a virtue in popular debates, but rather as a threat to the achievement of gender equality policy. Diversity and integration have thus become complex concepts within the Swedish intellectual and public debate, not least with the introduction of the notion of intersectionality. However, the debate on gender equality and diversity has not entirely entered the arena of policy decision making. The commission on structural discrimination did not, for example, form the grounds for any reforms or policies. Family and gender equality policies was formulated very much as it used to be when the government presented the future of gender equality policy in 2006, despite the talk on the need for intersectional analysis.

Gender equality policy towards new goals

In 2006, the first gender equality Bill in 12 years was presented (Bill 2005/06, no. 155). Taking its title from the government commission report preceding the Bill (*The Power to Shape Society and One's Own Life – New Goals in Gender Equality Policy*), it was again devised in collaboration with the Social Democratic, Green and Left Parties. The former Minister for Gender Equality Policy, Margareta Winberg, was replaced by the high-profile former journalist (and man), Jens Orback. However, even if a change of direction could be expected, Orback's discourse in presenting the goals for gender equality policy had an uncanny resemblance to Winberg's:

> Gender-equality policy is built on the feminist starting-point that there is an order or a social system in society which reproduces uneven power relations between the genders, where women are subordinatet and men superior as groups in society and where the man/the male constitutes the norm. Gender-equality policy aims to change this gender-power order and break the systematic subordination which means that women in general have a weaker social, economic, and political position in society than men, even though there are also differences within the groups of women and the groups of men. (Bill 2005/06, no. 155, pp 43-4)

There is, however, a subtle shift in discourse, visible towards the end of the quotation, indicating that the government acknowledges differences within social categories (such as gender); this deviation from the stern analytical focus on women's automatic subordinated position to men may indeed be seen as a harbinger of things to come. Although the relationship between women and men was still the primary setting for policy making, the overall aim of gender-equal policy was to 'provide for women and men to have the same power to shape society and their own lives' (Bill 2005/06, no. 155, p 43). This included 'all human beings … despite age, ethnicity, sexual orientation, disability or what region in the country one belongs to' (Bill 2005/06, no. 155, p 44). Thus, even if social categories such as ethnicity and disability were recognised, the overarching, dividing principle in society was still the one between women and men.

The overall aim had four sub-goals, all of which pledged allegiance to the gender equality goals established long before, building on the strategy of gender mainstreaming: an equal distribution of power and influence; lifelong economic equality between women and men; an equal distribution of unpaid household and caring work; and zero tolerance of men's violence against women.

The first sub-goal referred to aspects such as formal representation of women in public life and equal opportunities in society for girls and boys (through access to education, culture and mass media). It was also argued that the concept 'active citizenship' (*aktiva medborgare*) (proposed by the commission report preceding the Bill) should be changed to 'active citizens in society' (*aktiva samhällsmedborgare*). The reason for this was the government's assumption that the concept of citizenship could be used as an excluding mechanism for people born abroad or to those who were not Swedish citizens. In order to avoid the charge of exclusion, the concept of active citizens in society was launched, with the aim of achieving an 'inclusive, democratic idea of all women's and men's rights and possibilities to participation and influence in the development in society' (Bill 2005/06, no. 155, p 45).

The second sub-goal aimed to tackle economic inequality between women and men, and was all about equal rights for women and men to participate in education and paid work. Here, the notion of individual responsibility for breadwinning is central; that is, the goal set out to achieve equal opportunities for both women and men in the labour market, in order to facilitate economic independence for all.

The third sub-goal was defined as equal distribution of unpaid care work in the home. The most important goal was here to enable women and men to share unpaid labour in the home equally: 'It must be possible to unite gainful employment and to have a family' (Bill 2005/06, no. 155, p 49). Above all, this must be possible for both women and men.

The final sub-goal concerned men's violence against women, and the overarching aim here was to eliminate all violence against women.

In addition to these goals, the government proposed new steering principles for the gender equality policy field. It was proposed that gender mainstreaming as a strategy to achieve the gender equality policy goals was to be developed further.

Another question discussed in the Bill was the organisation of gender equality policy and gender mainstreaming. At the time, all (state-organised) gender equality work was carried out by the gender equality ombudsman (Jämställdhetsombudsmannen or JämO), the gender equality board and special advisers on county labour boards. Based on the critique against existing organisation (which was seen as inefficient), the government suggested an amalgamated arrangement – a central administrative agency for gender equality (Jämställdhetsmyndighet). It was thus suggested that the new agency should coordinate all gender equality work.

At the same time, another government commission (called the Committee of Discrimination) suggested that a new law against discrimination should replace the gender equality law and that the four existing anti-discrimination ombudsmen[2] should be replaced by one, new authority called the ombudsman against discrimination (SOU 2006:22). The aim was to 'introduce a more integrated Swedish law on discrimination', and to 'strengthen the human right perspective in Swedish law' (SOU 2006:22, p 214). The gender equality Bill, however, made it obvious that the government was not in favour of such an organisation. Instead, the government argued that it was important to separate the activities tied to the suggested gender equality authority and the one directed to prevent discrimination according to the law. It was, it argued, 'inappropriate that the same authority should support the work with gender mainstreaming at the same time as they should exercise supervision of laws' (Bill 2005/06, no. 155, p 64). One reason for the Committee of Discrimination's rejection of the proposal can perhaps be explained by the fact that the government considered integration policies as a field belonging to other policy fields (compare the statement that 'integration policies are carried out mainly within other policy fields' (Bill 2005/06, no. 155, p 90). Another explanation could be, as suggested earlier, that the government maintained the assumption that the gender power order was the primary principle for social hierarchies.

The aim of the government was to establish the new central administrative agency for gender equality in 2007. Just a few months after the government accepted the Bill, however, there was a general election in Sweden, and the social democrats lost power to a bourgeois government. The new gender equality authority was therefore never realised.

Centre-right family and gender equality policies

The social democrats fared badly in the 2006 election. In October 2006 a centre-right coalition (calling itself the alliance government and comprising the Moderate Party, the Liberal Party, the Centre Party and the Christian Democratic Party) came to power. Fredrik Reinfeldt of the Moderate Party was appointed prime minister.

The alliance government campaigned on the basis of the 'work line' – a classical social democratic theme reinvented by the centre-right parties in the mid-2000s. The Moderate Party went so far as to proclaim itself the 'New Labour Party – the New Moderates'. The most significant feature of the work line as championed by the alliance government is the supply–push measures of labour market policy to reduce marginalisation (*utanförskap*) and facilitate and increase labour market participation for all, including groups with weak or uneven interaction with the labour market. Family policy has been drawn into this reinvention of the work line, along similar lines to those in the 1960s, when activation was a key concept in labour market policy. Again, after a long period characterised by an outspoken gender mainstreaming approach, gender equality has clearly been subsumed by labour market policy. Several family policy reforms have been launched and these will be further investigated later.

The four government parties were, however, divided on the issue of family policy, as the Moderate Party and the Christian Democratic Party had traditionally upheld conservative values regarding the family and had vehemently opposed interventions in the family sphere. The Centre Party, and its ancestor the Agrarian Party, had taken a wide variety of positions, sometimes radical (in the 1940s) and later more closely related to that of the Moderate Party. The Liberal Party in turn had been a forceful proponent of radical family policy reform in the pursuit of gender equality.

The most conspicuous of the policy changes was the Moderate Party's family policy U-turn, culminating in Minister of Finance Anders Borg's revelation, made shortly before winning the election, that he was a 'feminist'. Inspired by Simone de Beauvoir, Borg articulated his worries in the media that his twin daughters would not have the same opportunities and life choices as boys. The gender power order, Borg argued, did not allow citizens to become free and independent; he claimed that 'gender roles that prevent and govern individual choice are a limitation of freedom' and this structure must be changed by political initiatives (*Expressen*, 13 March 2006). The welfare state, Borg continued, had created many structural obstacles for women in working life, but had also limited the incentives of men to use their entitlement to parental insurance. To achieve gender equality, these structures must be changed. When Borg was appointed Minister of Finance, he repeated his position: 'The definition of feminism is that there is a gender power order, and a wish to change this order. Since I share this opinion, and this is an idea that is closely connected to how I look upon freedom and people's equal value, I find it natural to call myself a feminist' (*SvD*, 14 January 2007). Feminism in practical (bourgeois) politics meant changing unequal structures in working life and in the family, especially with regard to unequal pay, differences in career paths and take-up of parental leave insurance.

Borg's position is not an anomaly. Representatives of the alliance government have repeatedly argued that gender inequalities have structural explanations and that policies should be devised to create equal conditions for women and men within the labour market. This has become something of a discursive thread in the alliance government, coexisting uneasily with the Christian Democratic Party's family policy agenda, where 'family support' and paid exit of housewives from the labour market feature prominently.

The following sections examine the alliance government's family policy and analyse the relationship – and possible antinomies – between different family policy strands. This not only marks the end of the historical narrative, but also illustrates some of the ambitions and paradoxes of Swedish family policy more generally.

Bourgeois family policy?

Continuity reigns in the alliance government's family policy discourse. As in virtually all areas, the government has been cautious and unwilling to make any radical departures from the established policy path. To achieve its goal, the government has outlined a four-pronged strategy:

- equal distribution of power and influence among men and women;
- economic equality;
- equal responsibility for unpaid household and caring labour;
- zero tolerance towards men's violence against women (Skr 2008/09:198, p 5).

The government also announced that it would retain the gender mainstreaming principles established in the mid-1990s. If continuity rather than change seemed to be the leitmotif of family policy, it must be noted that there were some important deviations from the established policy path. The first and perhaps most profound of these is the juxtaposition of freedom of choice and intervention:

> The government's ambition is that family policy should reinforce parents' power over their life situation and increase the freedom of choice for families. Family policy should facilitate the combination of work and family life for parents, through improved possibilities for both parents to participate in the labour market and to care for their children when they are young. The preconditions for gender equality must be improved. The government wants to enhance the freedom of choice for families by reducing the national political steering. Family policy should create good preconditions for families to cope with their everyday life according to their own desires and needs, and not force children and parents into politically dictated templates. (Bill 2007/08, no. 91, p 17)

These words, from the first family policy Bill in 2007, showed the family policy paradox within the alliance government: on the one hand, a dedicated stance towards (continued) reforms and steering mechanisms in relation to family and gender relations, and, on the other hand, an emphasis on self-determination and freedom of choice for families.

The tension between the two ambitions surfaced in a survey by the leading conservative daily *Svenska Dagbladet* in 2008 of the family policy reforms pursued so far and their impact on gender equality (*SvD*, 27 July 2008). The government itself had conducted an inquiry showing that parental responsibilities were unevenly divided between men and women. This was particularly evident when it came to child sick leave and reduced working hours for parents with small children; while 91% of fathers with small children worked full time, only 51% of women did so. The secretary of the Moderate Party, Per Schlingmann, claimed that this was the litmus test of gender equality – child sick leave tested whether 'the man's work and the man's meetings are more important than the woman's'.

Favouring stronger incentives over affirmative action and stronger public regulation, the government wanted to entice men to take on more household and caring responsibility, thereby increasing the supply of female labour in the workforce. The analysis is not very far removed from that of the previous social democratic government. Unequal relations within the family sphere, with women bearing the brunt of caring responsibility, made women more vulnerable in the labour market. Women fall behind men in terms of their careers and salaries. This vicious circle impedes labour market participation and thereby poses a threat to the funding of public welfare. The main difference between the alliance government and its social democratic predecessor is the former's firm belief in a combination of freedom of choice and political steering of women's (and men's) behaviour:

> Family policy must be concerned both with the creation of freedom and opportunities for families to find their own solution, and with strengthening women's position in the labour market. One reason behind wage discrimination is that women lose their position when the children grow up. A bonus, or an incentive system, can alleviate this. (Per Schlingmann, *SvD*, 27 July 2008)

The introduction of the cash-for-care scheme (*vårdnadsbidrag*) (discussed in more detail later), a *de facto* political concession to the Christian Democratic Party, is the epitome of the government's contradictory stance towards regulation. The allowance subsidises single-earner households, thereby counteracting the government's strategy of reducing the burden on dual-earner couples.

The issues addressed by the government – the uneven use of the parental insurance, the skewed distribution of part-time work and the inequalities of wage development – have recurred in political debates for decades, sometimes as far back as the 1930s. What is new this time? The government subscribes, to a certain extent, to the dominant analysis, but it adds its own twist to the remedy, primarily by focusing on economic incentives, one of which is the gender equality bonus.

The gender equality bonus system

Having discovered the unequal take-up of parental insurance among men and women – and the ensuing consequences for the position of women in the labour market – the alliance government set out to devise incentives for equality. The first of these was the equality bonus – a voluntary allowance organised by the municipalities with a maximum benefit of about 300 euros (3,000 kronor) per month – enacted in July 2008 (Bill 2007/08, no. 93). The allowance is tied to the family's use of parental insurance – the more even distribution between parents, the higher the benefit.

The bonus was explicitly presented as a reform to enhance gender equality, facilitate women's entry into the labour market and encourage fathers to stay at home with their children (2007/08:SfU10). The reform was preceded by a string of commission reports in which the government pledged to 'improve the preconditions for both men and women for taking an active and equal responsibility for parenthood, but without stripping families of their self-determination' (Ds 2007:50, p 7). Hence, the government is striking a balance between intervention and abstention, between respect for the autonomy of the family and measures to encourage men and women to divide family responsibilities equally (Ds 2007:50, p 7). The reform targeted not only the heterosexual nuclear family but also same-sex couples.

> Increasing gender equality can contribute to more secure family conditions and to more stable conditions for the children's upbringing as well as more equal conditions for working life careers for women and men. The reform means that the parent who has stayed at home the longest will receive a tax credit when she or he works and the other parent is supported by the parental insurance. The reform also makes it easier for parents of the same sex to share the parental leave equally. (Ds 2007:50, p 8)

While initial hopes were high, the outcome so far has been disappointing. In March 2010, the social insurance office (Försäkringskassan) reported that there had been no discernable impact on men's use of the parental insurance. Rather, it seemed as if most parents were ignorant of the bonus; those who knew about it considered it incomprehensible (Lövgren, 2010).

Another area of reform concerns the supply of labour. On 1 January 2007, the 'tax deduction on earned income' (*jobbskatteavdrag*) was introduced, reducing income taxes for those with gainful employment, but not those claiming unemployment insurance, parental insurance or social assistance.

Tax deduction on earned income was first outlined in 2005, in a parliamentary motion from the Moderate Party proposing that parental insurance should be supplemented with an 'employment deduction' scheme, giving spouses a tax reduction if their partner with a higher income stayed at home with the small children during their first year. The idea was to encourage high-income parents (normally men) to use their entitlement to parental insurance so as to enable mothers to return to work (motion 2005/6:m009, p 20). The combination aimed to create a greater supply of labour alongside equal 'caringhood' within families. In an example of the complexities of the alliance government's policies, the tax deduction on earned income ran parallel to the cash-for-care scheme, which had the opposite effect of enabling women to stay at home with their young children.

Cash-for-care scheme

A cash-for-care scheme was first introduced in 1994 by the then centre-right government. The scheme provided cash support of about 200 euros or 2,000 kronor per month to parents staying at home with children aged between one to three. However, after only a few months, the scheme was terminated by the social democrats, who won the 1994 election. In 2008, after its electoral victory, the alliance government resurrected the scheme, the aim being to 'create increased freedom of choice for parents wishing to spend more time with their small children', and to 'strengthen the parents' power over their life situation' (Bill 2007/08, no. 149, pp 14, 18). The scheme is different from that of 1994; it is no longer a national but a voluntary programme run and funded by the municipalities. Hence, it is the municipalities – and not the state – that decide whether or not to introduce the cash-for-care scheme, and hitherto only about one in four municipalities have done so. A condition of eligibility is that the child is not already covered by municipal childcare. Furthermore, the scheme cannot be combined with benefits from the parental insurance, unemployment insurance or health insurance schemes. It is, however, open to dual-income families with children in non-municipal childcare. In effect, the scheme supports not only women who stay at home with small children, but also parents who, for various reasons, do not use public childcare (Bill 2007/08, no. 91, p 17).

The antinomies of the family policy of the alliance government – whereby both parents are encouraged to work full time, but families also have the choice to determine whether to make use of the cash-for-care system and reduce their collective workload – was fiercely debated in parliament. The opposition, headed by the social democrats, was sceptical of the policy package, and instead proposed a prolongation of the parental insurance scheme as a way to improve gender equality. Furthermore, the policy pursued was seen as an attempt to hollow out public childcare, fostering instead a caring system comprising a combination of private childcare provision and housewives (Social Democratic motion no. 2007/08:Sf14 and Left Party motion no. 2007/08:Sf12). The cash-for-care scheme was also debated in parliament, where both the Left and Green Parties described it as an anomaly in relation to the work line (parliamentary protocol, 2008/09:47). However, the opposition parties failed in parliament and all the family policy reform programmes mentioned already have been implemented.

Strategies for a gender-neutral labour market

In its strategy for gender equality in the labour market and in the private sector, the alliance government stated not only that gender equality was one of its key goals but also that it contributed to economic growth 'by retaining and enabling the competence and creativity of people' (Skr. 2008/09:198, p 2). The government, however, conceded that working life is highly unequal, manifested in wage differentials, differences in career opportunities, incidences of work-related health problems and representation on company boards (Skr. 2008/09:198, p 3). The pattern of inequality in its turn undermines economic growth, calling for radical remedies, the government argued.

The following priorities were made: first, to counteract the gender division of labour in the labour market and in the private sector; second, to enhance female entrepreneurship; third, to level out gender differences in labour market participation; and fourth, to enact gender equality through legislation.

In order to reach these goals, a long list of practical measures was presented. To level out gender differences in education, for example, girls were encouraged to study science and both genders to make active educational choices without 'the constraints of stereotyped perceptions of gender' (Skr. 2008/09:198, p 33). Other measures included scrapping wealth taxation, reducing corporate taxation, lowering payroll taxes and reducing tax for household services, 'making it easier and more profitable to run a company' (Skr. 2008/09:198, p 35). The underlying assumption is that these reforms will facilitate female self-employment, which in turn is supposed to promote gender equality in the private sector. However, incentives were not the only path envisioned. Legislation, including a new anti-discrimination law (superseding the gender equality law and six other, related, laws), and the introduction of a new discrimination ombudsman (merging the former gender equality ombudsman and four other anti-discrimination ombudsmen roles) were also part of the government's gender equality arsenal. This organisational change, based on the suggestion made by the Commission for Discrimination (SOU 2006:22), led to the abolition of the gender equality Act from 1978 (changed in 1991). The ambition was to broaden the scope of equality policy, as the new ombudsman was also supposed to target 'multiple discrimination' (Skr. 2008/09:198, p 40). Moreover, the law was presented as a way of preventing discrimination (Bill 2007/08, no. 95). There was political consensus in relation to the introduction of the new discrimination law in general. However, the debates in parliament were extensive and highlighted the critique against some aspects of the law, partly directed towards gender equality as a ground for discrimination. The opposition was critical: the Left Party argued that the new law was too diffuse and unclear, proposing that an authority for gender equality be installed (Left Party motion to parliament, 2007/08:A8). The Green Party was positive, but, along with the Social Democratic Party, urged for clearer demands on gender equality plans and reinforced measures to bring about equal pay. The political opposition feared that the elements of its gender equality policies (such as the work on salary surveys and gender equality plans) would be downplayed by the new law:

> The gender equality law and JämO have been important parts in the ambition to install a gender equal society and to break the structural subordination women meet in the labour market. We do not want to see an impairment of this work in the new law on discrimination. (Social Democratic Party motion to parliament, 2007/08:A7)

Regulation of working life accounted for the bulk of the intervention package, where the equality bonus, tax reductions on household labour and stricter rules for sickness insurance (coupled with activation measures) were among the instruments intended to increase opportunities for women in the labour market. Realigning paid and unpaid labour was another key priority for the government, again to be stimulated through the equality bonus and tax cuts for 'household services'. The last point is of particular interest from the perspective of family policy:

> The tax reduction for household work will lead to more equal conditions for women and men to combine family life and working life. Women reduce their working hours to do household work to a greater extent than men. If women are given better possibilities to reallocate their time from household work to market-based work, their likelihood of earning higher incomes and participating in the labour market on equal terms will increase. (Skr. 2008/09:198, p 39; compare Bill 2006/07, no. 94)

The tax reduction scheme was subject to much criticism in parliament, along similar lines to the criticism of the cash-for-care scheme, namely that it cemented gender roles and reinforced class divisions in society. The social democrats argued that a reform that would lead to a situation where 'high-income women leave household work to – most likely – part-time, temporarily employed, low-income women is hardly a step forward for gender equality.... If the government really seriously wants to do something about the unfair division of labour within the household, steps must be taken to induce men to shoulder greater responsibilities for home and children' (motion no. 2006/07:Sk12). The Left Party concurred and argued that tax reduction on earned income relieved high-income men from taking responsibility for home and children and high-income women from confronting their spouses about these responsibilities (motion no. 2006/07:Sk10).

Family policy thus continues to be an issue of considerable ideological ferment, and it has been debated intensely over the past few years. However, the ideological disagreements have not concerned the goals – gender equality is now embraced by all political parties of any significance – but rather the means of achieving them.

Conclusion

Gender equality, diversity and work in the welfare state

Feminism came to the forefront of the debate on family and gender equality at the beginning of the new millennium. Women's position in society became a major political issue, gender equality rhetoric was used in election campaigns and almost all political parties claimed to be 'feminist'. At the same time, a new party entered the political arena – Feminist Initiative (F!). To respond to changing moods, and to pre-empt the political impact of F!, the social democratic government claimed to be a feminist government, with family and gender equality policies high on its political agenda. While feminism seemed to be on the brink of a real political breakthrough, it soon became the subject of conflict in mainstream policy debate, eventually curtailing the (radical) feminist promise. Nevertheless, state feminism and mainstream gender equality policy survived. Gender equality policy remains a central policy field, albeit in a less radical form than in the early 2000s.

The feminist explosion in the political landscape also brought another concept and social practice into the debate, namely diversification. By the end of the 1990s and the beginning of the 2000s, family and gender equality policies was heavily criticised for its alleged negligence of the experiences of migrant women and men. Feminists and post-colonial scholars opposed the government-sanctioned picture of Sweden as an international role model for gender equality. They argued that diversity was relevant only in efforts to integrate immigrants into so-called Swedish culture. The concept of diversity indeed seemed to function as a threat to the gender equality policy achievements that had been based on the notion of gender inequalities as the prime source of inequality in society.

When the social democrats were ousted in 2006, the incoming centre-right alliance government promised to increase employment and reduce labour market 'marginalisation'. One of the key priorities was to target women with small children and encourage them to increase their working hours. Women should undertake paid employment on equal terms with men, and this would be achieved through an array of incentives, including the equality bonus scheme to encourage the sharing of parental leave, support of female entrepreneurship to broaden the base of women in the top echelons of the economy, and tax deduction on earned income to encourage women to increase their working hours. The coherence of this policy mix has, however, been diluted by the cash-for-care scheme, which actively encourages women to stay at home with their children, at least until they reach the age of three. The alliance government has therefore reinvented the policy paradox of its centre-right predecessor in the 1990s, with clashing incentives to work and to stay at home for women with small children.

Care work in the adult worker model

Care work has continued to focus on shared responsibility between women and men for children and household tasks. Inevitably, the organisation of care work has also become an issue for non-nuclear families, not least since the right of homosexual couples to adopt children and the right of lesbians to access donor insemination in the public healthcare system were enacted.

Despite the Swedish circumscribed neoliberalism, a string of family policy reforms have been introduced in recent years by social democrats and alliance parties alike. This includes a system of maximum fees for childcare, with the explicit aim of encouraging parents to work full time. The parental insurance scheme was extended and a 'daddy quota' of two months introduced. These reforms all reflect earlier ambitions to include in family policy making attempts to encourage men to shoulder caring responsibilities. Thus, family policy remained heavily influenced by masculinity research in an attempt to transform men into caring fathers. Gender equality policy for its part applied arguments about the structural subordination of women and aimed to empower women in working life, within the political system, in the public sector and in the corporate hierarchies.

The alliance government continued on the well-trodden path of gender equality policy, but added its own quirks to the policy mixture. In family policy, the change of direction showed primarily in the regulation of unpaid (care) work. By enforcing tax reductions for household work, the government intended to relocate unpaid housework into the market, with the assumption that gender equality could be achieved if household work was commodified (and government subsidised). Instead of relying solely on the state – as in the 1960s and the 1970s, when it was argued that (all) women could be released from their caring duties by expanding the public sector – the market became a gender equality instrument, serving to share the responsibilities for care work between families to release (middle-class) women from the burden of unpaid labour. At the same time, the alliance government introduced the cash-for-care-scheme, which – paradoxically it may seem – incentivised women to return to the family sphere. The only possible explanation for this paradox is that the measures are aimed at different groups of women – affluent and poor, 'Swedes' and migrants.

Another theme in the politics of care relates to homosexual parents. Interestingly, politics on homosexuality does not articulate with the mainstream of gender equality policy goals; homosexual relations are not even considered therein. Such matters are relegated to another policy field, that of sexual politics. This policy dichotomy – yet another paradox in family policy – became obvious in the debate on homosexual couples' right to adoption. Gender equality policy has as a core ambition to highlight and counteract gender differences. The political regulation of homosexual parenthood instead elevates the difference between women and men to a virtue – the heterosexual couple, with its distinct male–female roles, becomes the examplar, while the homosexual couple is at fault for failing to display the (otherwise challenged) distinct gender roles attributed to the traditional nuclear family. Thus, legal rights for homosexual couples rest on the assumption that homosexuality is a contradiction of the heterosexual family ideal.

Notes

[1] The law on registered partnership was abolished in 2009 and replaced by a new law on gender-neutral marriage. From 1 May 2009, a person's gender was no longer significant as far as marriage was concerned. Same-sex couples could get married and share the same rights as married, heterosexual couples.

[2] The four ombudsmen were the gender equality ombudsman, the ombudsman against ethnic discrimination, the disability ombudsman and the ombudsman against discrimination because of sexual orientation. The new law included discrimination against sex, transgender identity or expression, ethnicity, religion or other belief, disability, sexual orientation or age.

SEVEN

Conclusion: family policy paradoxes

This study examines the political regulation of the family in Sweden between 1930 and 2010, a period where a relationship has always existed between gender equality ideology and family policies to a greater or lesser extent, and where the two have sometimes even overlapped or have become mutually reinforcing. Despite this, the relationship has been complicated both to establish and to describe. The history of the Swedish family is therefore not one of linear progress from gender inequality to shared responsibilities under the auspices of the state, but rather one of false starts and contradictions between different and sometimes incompatible interests and goals. It is a history marked by policy paradoxes, of male–breadwinner ideals colliding with labour market demands, of individual emancipation clashing with role conservatism, of gender inequalities in the home and in the labour market, and of the gendered division of care work in the changing organisation of the welfare state, the market and the family.

This chapter returns to the major elements in the way Sweden has articulated and resolved these family policy paradoxes, with the aim of illustrating how they may be used to inform the hotly debated issue of balancing work and family commitments in contemporary Europe.

Modern family policy emerged in the early 1930s as an offshoot of population policy, a central policy area and a major political concern at the time. Without the massive interest in the 'population question', the family would probably not have been constituted as an object of political intervention.

The direction and content of family policy were transformed in the process, targeting the family as an organic unit. With the rise of new perspectives in population policy grounded in family sociology, the form and function of the family emerged as a key element in the 'population question'. If the population question were ever to be 'solved', family formation and family development had to be embedded in a framework of public policies. The most poignant formulation of the new stance towards the family was Alva Myrdal and Gunnar Myrdal's (1934) *Crisis in the Population Question*, which encapsulated a new spirit of interventionism in family policy. The family was moving out of the private sphere, becoming instead an object of public intervention.

The interventionist tendency was reinforced by the political interest in the family beyond the confines of population politics. Family issues resonated well with other nascent policy fields where the social conditions for families were a matter of great urgency. One of the first reform fields pertaining to the social conditions for families was housing, where poverty and shortage of space among large families with children propelled the emergence of the social housing policy.

The ambition set for family policy was threefold: increasing fertility, stabilising family formation (and gender relations) and enhancing the economic conditions for families with children. Declining fertility levels were tackled through measures such as improved motherhood care and increased access to delivery care. Even though the reforms were modest and motherhood insurance retained its residualism and meagre benefits, they were the first steps towards political intervention in reproduction, ground-breaking steps with long-lasting repercussions. Securing the conditions for women in the labour market was another element, which manifested itself both in legal regulation against dismissing women on the basis of marital status, pregnancy and household responsibilities and in a general debate on the preconditions for female employment. A decisive point in this respect was whether the measures taken should be voluntary or compulsory, and opposing views were presented by different factions of the influential government commission system. In the end, a legal route, advocated by the powerful population commission, became the model for policy interventions. Finally, child allowance became the primary measure for economic security.

Family policy partly developed out of population policy and as a new solution to the pressing 'population question', but its articulation in another policy domain, the labour market, was becoming increasingly important. Women were conceived not only as 'mothers' and caretakers, but also as labour market participants. This marked the first formulation of the paradox of Swedish family policy, the antinomical relationship between work and family, only half acknowledged in political debates. The parallel debates and policy practices were sometimes interconnected, for instance in parliamentary debates on the reach and eligibility criteria of family policy measures. Such debates highlighted the interplay between reproduction and work and the balance between universalism and residualism in social policy intervention more generally. New paradoxes were forthcoming; as the social democratic government did not want to provoke opposition to 'women-friendly' reforms, it tried to strike a balance between tradition and renewal by introducing somewhat residual measures rather than an inclusive motherhood insurance system. This, in turn, meant that the reach of family policy was still limited.

Family policy not only had a regulatory dimension; it also concerned the inner life and mechanisms of the family. Difficulties in sexual relationships emerged as a key explanation behind the population crisis, with widespread 'rationalised' sexual attitudes hampering fertility. On the other hand – and here we find another paradox – rationality had not gone far enough in other respects, as indicated by the spread of venereal diseases, which could be remedied through educational programmes. Yet another paradox concerned the quality of fertility, as the social distribution of fertility was seen as skewed; fertility levels among certain groups in society were thought to be *too high*, for instance among poor people and the 'mentally retarded'. In addition, it was argued that those women deemed to be 'worn-out' or 'nervous' should be prevented from having more children. The quality of the population was as important as its quantity, and skewed fertility had to be corrected, with a larger share reserved for healthy women and men. The contradiction between levels of fertility that were either too high or too low was to be resolved by drastic measures, including the sterilisation of 'unfit' women and men, and social and economic incentives for those deemed fit to raise a family.

This was an era where efficiency and rationalisation were cherished in all areas of society, from industrial production to marital relations, and the family was, of course, drawn into this broad project. Sexuality, in particular, was perceived to be a hotbed of traditional and unenlightened attitudes, ripe for reform. Family policy intervention could not stop at the gates of the household but had to reform gender relations if the population question were ever to be solved. This was at least the argument put forward in radical debates like the Myrdals', and family policy therefore emerged as a spearhead in the modernisation of Swedish society. While powerful in its discourse, this line of argument was more modest in its practical outcome. The main impact was in motherhood insurance and the development of motherhood and paediatric care. This resulted in a policy field directed towards women only and equality goals within the family policy field became equated with women's position in society.

The family was drawn into the modernisation of Swedish society, primarily at the level of discourse where public intellectuals like the Myrdals joined forces with the government commissions against conservative social and political interests wanting to shield the family from political intervention. The government commissions were particularly important as platforms for the nascent field of social studies of families but also as test sites and early think-tanks for policy interventions into the form and function of families. The commissions thus combined the roles of knowledge producers, discursive forums/think-tanks and arenas for political deliberations on the direction of family policy.

The end of the Second World War marked the beginning of the 'harvest time'. When the fears of a post-war depression (articulated by, for instance, Gunnar Myrdal) turned out to be overstated, the manoeuvring space for social policy became much larger than was initially expected. The three areas of social policy expansion were basic security, income support and social services. The initial focus was on basic security and the elimination of poverty in society. The flagship reform was the introduction of child allowance, a first step in the sharing of costs for children between families and state. Surprisingly, child allowance was introduced with bipartisan support; justice arguments motivated the parties of the left, while concerns about national security (military preparedness) and reproduction motivated the bourgeois parties. Consequently, child allowance temporarily united different perspectives on the family. However, it would not be long before tensions and contradictions again shaped family policy debate and practice, one example being the retraction of the proposed expansion of motherhood insurance soon after the child allowance had been introduced.

The population question was still an important framework for family policy initiatives and reform, where declining fertility and its causes and consequences was delegated to a new population commission covering everything from housing to sexual education. As mentioned, some reforms had already been initiated to redress the imbalance between caring obligations and labour market participation. Paradoxical stances towards the family kept appearing; in some reforms the notion of the nourishing and caring mother was fundamental to the future of Swedish society, while in others, women's conditions in the labour market were paramount. Such ambivalent ideals shaped family policy paradoxes well into the 1960s, and to some extent continue to shape the family policy mix.

The government commission system was a battleground for contradictory family policy ideals. One report (SOU 1947:46), shaped by nuclear family ideals in both its analysis and prescriptions, idealised a strict division of labour within the family, where women took the responsibility for caring and for consumption while men were producers and represented the family in the labour market. The report, drawing on contemporary family studies of a structural-functionalist bent, investigated family environment, housing organisation and the distribution of economic responsibilities between the spouses, as well as how sexual and emotional relations within a 'modern marriage' could secure sound reproduction and balanced family ideals in a turbulent society.

Hence, the nuclear family was seen as a historical victory in need of careful public support and guidance. In other policy circumstances, other ideals pervaded. In the 1950s, when the supply of labour was becoming increasingly scarce, an increase in the provision of state childcare was suggested as a public obligation to support and sustain female employment. Hence, and as a sharp contrast to the elevation of the nuclear family, women's employment became a topical issue and there were calls for public interventions to reduce the pressure on working women. Not only, experts argued, would the urgent need for more labour power be satisfied if state childcare were expanded, but also women would find their position in the labour market strengthened and their identity as employers reinforced. This position could find support in modern psychological and sociological studies showing that women were torn between the 'two roles' of mother and employee. The tensions could no longer be suppressed or denied, forcing public authorities to intervene to reconcile the two roles. This would not only reduce the pressure on women, but would also provide children with more variety and broaden their perspective beyond the confines of the home.

The conclusion drawn – not surprisingly in a report from another government commission (SOU 1951:15) – was that state childcare had to be radically expanded, and funded and run by both the state and the municipalities (childcare had hitherto often been organised by charities). These were radical proposals, difficult to digest in their contemporary political setting, but that does not imply that they were meaningless expressions of political radicalism. They articulated a growing societal tension – between the need to increase the supply of labour and the rigidities of family organisation – and paved the way for forthcoming initiatives. Slowly but steadily, the family policy discourse incorporated the view that women were in need of an identity based not only on caring and household work but also on gainful employment. All of this paved the way for the weak male-breadwinner model, where the sharp demarcations in responsibilities between the genders were modified if not thoroughly transformed. The rising demand for labour and the identification of women as an important labour market reserve was more evidence of the potential for women's 'two roles'.

Ambivalence, and sometimes outright paradox, shaped family policy in the immediate post-war period; the nuclear family and the male-breadwinner model were elevated as family policy ideals at the same time as it was argued that women and children should be (partially) released from the tight grip of the family by gainful employment and the provision state childcare.

This unresolved paradox exploded in the 1960s, when a profound reorientation of family policy came to fruition. It began with a change in the academic discourse, where the focus on the nuclear family was more or less eradicated. It was superseded by the sex-role debate, that obligations in the household and in the labour market were constructed and therefore subject to change. Sex roles were not rooted in 'natural' or biological traits. Thus the responsibilities of caring, for which women had hitherto been portrayed as the protagonists because of what had been perceived as natural/biological reasons, were ripe for transformation, involving men on an equal footing with women. The balanced, gender-equal family became a lead theme in family policy, and family policy reforms were guided by a gender-neutral ideal. Material motives also inspired the gender neutrality debate, as the growing demand for labour continued and the relationship between household and labour market organisation was subjected to increasing scrutiny.

Changes in the political landscape added to the reorientation of family policy, as the Social Democratic and Liberal Parties competed for gender equality hegemony. At its 1969 congress, the Social Democratic Party presented the report *Equality* (*Jämlikhet*, 1969), arguably one of the first political documents promoting gender-neutral family policy and a sign of a decisive break with the nuclear family ideals of 1950s and early 1960s family policy. Justice and freedom of choice were the central goals, pitted against the confines of stereotypical sex roles. The route to human emancipation – not only for women but also for men – was through reforms to taxation (from joint to individual tax) and changes in family law and in labour market policy. Men, arguably for the first time, were explicitly targeted by family policy, as evidenced, for instance, by the replacement of maternity insurance with a new gender-neutral parental insurance scheme. Women and men were supposed to share the responsibility for caring and for the family income. Combined roles in the household and in the labour market would, it was suggested, create a gender-equal and women-friendly society.

While the responsibility for caring was a central theme in the debate, the family policy practice shifted towards labour market conditions, primarily through intense efforts to bring about gender equality in the workplace. A string of gender equality agreements and laws for the public and private sector were enacted, and later working hours for parents with small children were shortened. In 1979, omnibus legislation on gender discrimination was introduced through the gender equality Act. In general, the 1970s was a decade of workplace reform in Sweden, and this had a knock-on effect on gender equality policy as the focus on gender relations within the family subsided. Gender equality was, it was argued, critically dependent on reformed relations in the workplace.

This would soon change. An emerging feminist critique challenged hegemonic notions of caring responsibilities and 'sex roles', a debate that had receded in the 1970s. Another issue that had virtually disappeared by the 1970s was differences. The gender-neutral discourse had constructed the interests of women, men and children as similar, under the umbrella of 'everybody's needs' of gender equality, thereby obscuring the differences that remained under the gender equality façade.

Again, it was the government commissions that initiated the discursive break, this time through surveys of the state of equality in Swedish society at the onset of the 1980s. The surveys were highly critical of the impact of family and gender equality policies, as little had been achieved in the distribution of caring responsibilities. As women were still the primary carers, their position in the labour market and more generally in society was far weaker than men's. The impressive array of reforms and agreements had not had a major impact on the distribution of power between women and men; only in their overt manifestations in the workplace had uneven gender relations even begun to be challenged. Gender equality policy was thus seen as a failure.

One explanation for the family paradox at the time, whereby gender equality and gender neutrality were promoted in legislation and gender segregation in family practice, was the severe economic crisis of the late 1970s and the emergence of neoliberal politics in the 1980s. This reduced the space for further reforms of gender relations. Another explanation was the time it took for reforms to have an effect. Reforms in the 1960s had been preoccupied with the transition from single-earner households to double-income families (or from a strong to a weak male-breadwinner model). The equalisation of economic conditions had barely been achieved by the early 1980s, when the time then seemed ripe for a reconsideration of the impact of this transition on gender relations. The cognitive foundations for family policy had also changed when gender neutrality and sex roles were superseded by a focus on power relations and the different interests of women and men. Women's needs were again emphasised, and men's role in the uneven distribution of caring responsibilities was emphasised; men as a group had not done their share of caring and household work, which reproduced traditional inequalities. Men and unpaid work became the subject of the new field of 'daddy politics'. This line of argument was taken up in family policy, which by then had gone through three phases, first focusing on women within the family, then on gender neutrality and finally on men's role as carers.

The issue raised concerned the impact of gender-neutral measures on a society that was not gender neutral. A much-discussed government commission on women's representation argued that voluntary measures had not served gender equality well enough and that the time was ripe for more radical measures such as gender quotas and affirmative action. While this radical proposal, like other radical proposals before it, was discarded, it played a central role in the 1991 election, not least because of the impact of the Support Stockings (Stödstrumporna) prior to the election. The theoretical inspiration behind the debate was the influential gender systems analysis, suggesting that women as a group were structurally subordinated to men. Power aspects were becoming increasingly important in the debates on remaining gender inequalities in Sweden, and so were the consequences of the defamiliarisation process, which called for the individualisation of the social insurance system. In order to achieve gender equality in these new circumstances, reforms were twofold.

On the one hand, women's representation should be enhanced, women should be compensated for structural discrimination (a politics 'in favour of women') and violence against women should be combated. Some early attempts at gender mainstreaming were also made, whereby all policy areas were to incorporate a gender equality perspective. All this shaped the gender equality policy of the 1990s. The reformulation of gender equality policy also marked a reconsideration of the alleged women-friendliness of the Swedish welfare state.

On the other hand, family policy reforms and debates were directed at fathers and at attempts to include them in unpaid care work. 'Daddy politics' became an even more important field after the election in 1991, when a centre-right government took power. While the government made a virtue of breaking up the post-war policy consensus, gender equality was not subject to the same political turmoil as other policy fields. Instead, the new government built on similar ideas as its predecessor, namely that women were structurally subordinated to men. It went further than the social democratic government, however, fully establishing gender mainstreaming, reforming parental insurance by introducing gender quotas (the so-called daddy month) and sharpening the gender equality Act. This impinged on the system of collective bargaining, as gender equality was now enforced by law rather than by agreement, pitting gender equality against one of the key elements of the Swedish model – voluntary agreements in the labour market. At the same time, the introduction of the cash-for-care scheme (which was the result of a compromise between the liberals and the Christian Democratic Party) was in itself another family policy paradox and remains so today. Simultaneously emphasising women's participation in the labour market and incentivising women to stay at home is indeed a contradiction in terms.

Gender mainstreaming was first mentioned in the gender equality Bill of the centre-right government in 1994 and was taken up by its social democratic successor in 1995 – again indicating the path-dependency of gender equality policy. Also, again seeking inspiration in studies of gender inequalities, the term 'gender power order' was enrolled in gender equality policy and thereby also in family policy, indicating the radicalisation of gender equality and family policy by the end of the 1990s.

The social democratic government proclaimed itself to be 'feminist' at the beginning of the 2000s and set about to combat the gender power order according to which men were superior to women; furthermore, it adhered to a social constructivist account of gender relations, viewing gender patterns as mirrors of upbringing, culture, economic conditions, power structures and ideologies.

These convictions were to shape and influence family policy priorities, to some extent as a countermeasure to the rise of the feminist party Feminist Initiative (F!), which received massive support in its early phase (after negative publicity focusing on internal conflicts, F! lost much of its influence).

The emphasis on gender equality as a specifically Swedish (or sometimes Nordic) virtue propelled a critical debate about the difficulty of including the experiences of certain groups, particularly migrant women (and men). The debate was sparked off when Sweden was celebrated by the social democratic family policy elite as the world's most gender-equal society with a unique 'culture of gender equality'. Critics argued that gender equality policies ignored ethnicity and the intersection between different forms of subordination, and that the very basis of the gender equality ambition rested on cultural essentialism, resulting in structural discrimination. To some extent the critique has been adopted in policy making, where a broader and more encompassing understanding of rights now forms the basis for politics and policy against discrimination, putting gender equality on a par with ethnic and sexual rights.

The social democratic government in power between 1994 and 2006 continued the alliance with the gender power analysis, and devised policies according to this rather peculiar interpretation of the inequalities of gender relations. The gender policy discourse was vociferous but the measures taken were more modest. If anything, the social democratic government was less radical in its gender equality reforms than its centre-right predecessor, even though its family policy made some headway, in areas such as the introduction of a maximum childcare fee, which played a decisive role in the 2002 election campaign.

The centre-right government, elected in 2006, treads on the same gender equality path as its predecessors. It holds a strong belief in the virtues of combining freedom of choice and political intervention in women's (and men's) behaviour. In this sense, it embodies the paradoxes of Swedish family throughout the post-war period, enforcing ambitious policy goals while at the same time cherishing the independence and autonomy of women and men (although, for the alliance government, independence and autonomy are closely intertwined with neoliberal ideas).

Indeed, the government actively promotes the image of continuity by adhering to the work line (a concept first introduced by the labour movement in the 1940s). Full employment and maximum labour market participation have been set as the overarching goals, with repercussions on family policy priorities. Several measures have been introduced to influence gender relations so as to enhance women's positions in the labour market, for instance an increase in the gender quota and the introduction of an equality bonus in parental insurance. In order to solve the care work dilemma for women, the alliance government introduced tax incentives to discourage women from staying at home and encourage what was referred to as market-based work, resulting in the reintroduction of class politics in gender equality and family policy. However, and as a concession to the Christian Democratic Party (and to the ideal of freedom of choice), the cash-for-care system has been re-established to support stay-at-home mothers and to support private day-care provision. A significant change is that the idea of a gender power order has been discarded, as the government subscribes to a wider definition of subordination, and it has included 'multiple discrimination' in anti-discrimination laws.

The final paradox may not be a paradox at all, namely that family policy, unlike virtually all other policy fields, is not subject to ideological contestation or struggle. Few if any policy areas show such continuity as family policy (and later on gender equality policy); changes in government and ideological thinking seem to have little impact on the hegemony and path dependency of the gender equality discourse and policy practice. Social democratic and centre-right governments alike argue that gender inequalities have a detrimental impact not only on women and men (and children), but also on society as a whole and on employment and economic growth. Thus, women and men must share caring and household responsibilities. Gender equality is in policy rhetoric and discourse the key to building a wealthy and sustainable society, and this conviction has become something of a dogma in Swedish politics. This is likely to hold true for the foreseeable future.

References

[order transposed, have begun with authored publications; translations needed?]

Abukhanfusa, K. (1987) 'Kvinnorna i välfärdssamhället', in G. Kyle (ed) *Handbok i kvinnohistoria*, Stockholm: Carlssons, pp 137-62.

Acker, J., Baude, A., Björnberg, U., Dahlström, E., Forsberg, G., Gonäs, L., Holter, H. and Nilsson, A. (eds) (1992) *Kvinnors och mäns liv och arbete*, Stockholm: SNS förlag.

Ahlberg, J., Roman, C. and Duncan, S. (2008) 'Actualizing the "democratic family"? Swedish policy rhetoric versus family practices', *Journal of Social Politics*, vol 15, no 1, pp 79-100.

Axelsson, C. (1991) *Hemmafrun som försvann. Övergången till lönearbete bland gifta kvinnor.* Stockholm: Institutet för social forskning.

Åkerman, B. (1994) *88 år på 1900-talet. Bland vänner och idéer*, Stockholm: T. Fischer & Co.

Åkerman, B. (1945) *Gammal och ny familj*, Stockholm: Kooperativa kvinnogilleförbundet (stencil).

Ålund, A. (2000) 'Etnicitetens mångfald och mångfaldens etnicitet', in E. Olsson (ed) *Etnicitetens gränser och transnationella gemenskap*, Stockholm: Carlssons bokförlag.

Ålund, A. and Schierup, C.-U. (1991) *Paradoxes of Multiculturalism: Essays on Swedish Society*, Aldershot: Avebury.

Åmark, K. (1998) *Solidaritetens gränser: LO och industriförbundsprincipen under 1900-talet*, Stockholm: Atlas.

Åmark, K. (2005) *Hundra år av välfärdspolitik: Välfärdsstatens framväxt i Norge och Sverige*, Umeå: Boréa Bokförlag.

Anttonen, A. and Sipilä, SJ (1996) 'European social care services: is it possible to identify models?', *Journal of European Social Policy*, vol 6, no 2, pp 87-100.

Åsling, N. (1979) *Maktkamp eller samförstånd: En studie i svensk realpolitik.* Stockholm: LTs förlag.

Åström, G. (1990) 'Föräldraförsäkring och vårdnadsbidrag – om förhållandet mellan ideology och verklighet', *Kvinnovetenskaplig tidskrift*, vol 11, no 2, pp 37-49.

Baude, A. (ed) (1992) *Visionen om jämställdhet*, Stockholm: SNS förlag.

Barrett, M. and McIntosh, M. (1982) *The Anti-Social Family*, London: Verso.

Beck, U. (1992) *Risk Society: Towards a New Modernity*, London: Sage Publications.

Beck, U. (2002) *Individualization: Institutionalized Individualism and its Social and Political Consequences*, London: Sage Publications.

Beck, U. and Beck-Gernsheim, E. (1995) *The Normal Chaos of Love*, London: Polity Press.

Beck-Gernsheim, E. (2002) *Reinventing the Family: In Search of New Lifestyles*, Cambridge: Polity Press.

Benner, M. (1997) *The Politics of Growth: Economic Regulation in Sweden, 1930–1994*, Lund: Arkiv förlag.

Benner, M. and Vad, T. (2000) 'Sweden and Denmark', in F. Scharpf and V. Schmidt (eds) *Welfare and Work in the Open Economy Vol. II: Diverse Responses to Common Challenges in Twelve Countries*, Oxford: Oxford University Press.

Bergman, H. and Hobson, B. (2002) 'Compulsory fatherhood: the coding of fatherhood in the Swedish welfare state', in B. Hobson (ed) *Making Men into Fathers: Men, Masculinities and the Social Politics of Fatherhood*, Cambridge: Cambridge University Press, pp 92-125.

Bergqvist, C. (ed) (1999) *Equal Democracies: Gender and Politics in the Nordic Countries*, Oslo: Scandinavian University Press in co-operation with the Nordic Council of Ministers.

Beveridge, W. (1942) *Social Insurance and Allied Services*, London: HMSO.

Björnberg, U. and Kollind, A.-K. (2003) *Att leva själv tillsammans: Jämställdhet, autonomi och gemenskap i parrelationer*, Malmö: Liber.

Bock, G. and Thane, P. (1991) *Maternity and Gender Policies: Women and the Rise of the European Welfare States 1880s–1950s*, London and New York, NY: Routledge.

Borchorst, A. (2004) 'Skandinavisk ligestillingspolitik tur-retur, på dansk billet', *Nytt Norsk Tidskrift*, no 3-4, pp 264-74.

Borchorst, A. (2008) 'Woman-friendly policy paradoxes? Childcare policies and gender equality visions in Scandinavia', in K. Melby, A.-B. Ravn and C. Carlsson Wetterberg (eds) *Gender Equality and Welfare Politics in Scandinavia*, Bristol: The Policy Press.

Borchorst, A. (2009) 'Scandinavian gender equality: competing discourses and paradoxes', FREIA Paper No. 69, Aalborg: Aalborg University.

Borchorst, A. and Siim, B. (1987) 'Women and the advanced welfare state: a new kind of patriarchal power', in S. Sasson (ed) *Women and the State*, London: Hutchinson.

Borchorst, A. and Siim, B. (2009) 'Woman-friendly policies and state feminism: theorizing Scandinavian gender equality', *Feminist Theory*, vol 9, no 2, pp 207-24.

Broberg, G. and Roll-Hansen, N. (1996) *Eugenics and the Welfare State: Sterilization Policy in Denmark, Sweden, Norway, and Finland*, East Lansing, MI: Michigan State University Press.

Burgess, E. and Locke, H.J. (1945) *The Family: From Institution to Companionship* (2nd edn), New York, NY: American Books Company.

Carbin, M. (2008) 'Honour related violence. The invention of a policy problem in Sweden', in E. Magnusson, M. Rönnblom and H. Silius (eds) *Critical Studies of Gender Equality. Nordic Dislocation, Dilemmas and Contradictions*, Stockholm: Makadam.

Carlsson, C. (1986) *Kvinnosyn och kvinnopolitik: En studie av svensk socialdemokrati 1880-1910*, Lund: Arkiv förlag.

Carlsson Wetterberg, C. (1992) 'Från patriarkat till genussystem – och vad kommer sedan?', *KVT*, vol 15, no 2, pp 34-48.

Christiansen, N.F., Petersen, K., Edling, N. and Haave, P. (eds) (2006) *The Nordic Model of Welfare: A Historical Reappraisal*, Copenhagen: Museum Tusculanum Press.

Crompton, R. (1999) *Restructuring Gender Relations and Employment: The Decline of the Male Breadwinner Model*, Oxford: Oxford University Press.

Crompton, R. (2006) *Employment and the Family. The Reconfiguration of Work and Family Life in Contemporary Society*, Cambridge: Cambridge University Press.

Dahlerup, D. (1998) *Rødstrumperne: Den danske Rødstrumpebevægelses udvikling, nytænkning og gennemslag, 1970-1985*, Copenhagen: Gyldendal.

Dahlström, C. (2004) 'Rhetoric, practice and the dynamics of institutional change. Immigrant policy in Sweden 1964-2000', *Scandinavian Political Studies*, vol 27, no 3 , pp 287-310.

Dahlström, E. et al (1962) *Kvinnors liv och arbete: Svenska och norska studier av ett aktuellt samhällsproblem*, Stockholm: Prisma.

Daly, M. (2000) *The Gender Division of Welfare: The Impact of the British and German Welfare States*, Cambridge: Cambridge University Press.

Daly, M. (2005) 'Gender mainstreaming in theory and practice', *Social Politics*, vol 12, no 3, pp 433-50.

Daly, M. and Lewis, J. (2000) 'The concept of social care and the analysis of contemporary welfare states', *British Journal of Sociology*, vol 51, no 2, pp 281-98.

Daly, M. and Rake, K. (2001) *Gender and the Welfare State: Care, Work and Welfare in Europe and the USA*, Cambridge: Polity Press.

de los Reyes, P., Molina, I. and Mulinari, D. (eds) (2002) *Maktens (o)lika förklädnader: Kön, klass och etnicitet i det postkoloniala Sverige*, Stockholm: Atlas.

Edenheim, S. (2005) *Begärets lagar. Moderna statliga utredningar och heteronormativitetens genealogi*, Stockholm: Symposion.

Edlund, S. (1989) 'Saltsjöbadsavtalet i närbild', in S. Edlund, A.L. Johansson, R. Meidner, K. Misgeld and S. Nilsson (eds) *Saltsjöbadsavtalet 50 år: Forskare och parter begrundar en epok 1938–1988*, Stockholm: Arbetslivscentrum.

Elgán, E. (1994) *Genus och politik. En jämförelse mellan svensk och fransk abort- och preventivmedelspolitik från sekelskiftet till andra världskriget*, Uppsala: Studia Historica Upsaliensia 176.

Ellingsæter, A.-L. (1998) 'Dual breadwinner societies: provider models in the Scandinavian welfare states', *Acta Sociologica*, vol 41, no 59, pp 40-73.

Ellingsæter, A.-L. and Leira, A. (eds.) (2006) *Politicising Parenthood in Scandinavia. Gender Relations in Welfare States*, Bristol: The Policy Press.

Ellingsæter, A.-L. and Leira, A. (eds) (2007) *Velferdsstaten og familien: Utfordringer og dilemmaer*, Oslo: Gyldendal.

Elvander, N. (1972) *Svensk skattepolitik 1945-1970: En studie i partiers och organisationers funktioner*, Stockholm: Rabén & Sjögren.

Esping-Andersen, G. (1990) *The Three Worlds of Welfare Capitalism*, Cambridge: Polity Press.

Esping-Andersen, G. (ed) (2002) *Welfare States in Transition: National Adaptations in Global Economies*, London: Sage Publications.

Fink, J. and Lundqvist, Å. (eds) (2009) *Välfärd, genus och familj*, Malmö: Liber.

Fink, J. and Lundqvist, Å. (eds) (2010) *Changing Relations of Welfare. Family, Gender and Migration in Britain and Scandinavia*, Aldershot: Ashgate.

Florin, C. (1999) 'Skatten som befriar: hemmafruar mot yrkeskvinnor i 1960-talets särbeskattningsdebatt', in C. Florin, L. Sommestad and U.Wikander (eds) *Kvinnor mot kvinnor: Om systerskapets svårigheter*, Stockholm: Norstedts.

Florin, C. and Karlsson, B. (2000) *Någonting som liknar en oblodig revolution: Jämställdhetens politisering under 1960- och 1970-talen*, Umeå: Umeå University.

För barnens skull (1993) Stockholm: Regeringens pappagrupp/Socialdepartementet.

Frangeur, R. (1998) *Yrkeskvinna eller makens tjänarinna: Striden om yrkesrätten för gifta kvinnor i mellankrigstidens Sverige*, Lund: Arkiv förlag.

Fraser, N. (2007) *Justice Interruptus: Critical Reflections in the 'Postsocialist' Condition*, London: Routledge.

Giddens, A. (1991) *Modernity and Self-Identity: Self and Society in the Late Modern Age*, Cambridge: Polity Press.

Giddens, A. (1992) *The Transformation of Intimacy: Sexuality, Love and Eroticism in Modern Societies*, Cambridge: Polity Press.

Gordon, L. (1988) *Heroes of Their Own Lives: The Politics and History of Family Violence, Boston, 1880–1960*, New York: Viking.

Hammar, T. (1999) 'Closing the doors to the Swedish welfare state', in G. Brochmann and T. Hammar *Mechanisms of Immigration Control. A Comparative Analysis of European Regulation Policies*, Oxford: Berg Publisher.

Hantrais, L. (2004) *Family Policy Matters: Responding to Family Change in Europe*, Bristol: The Policy Press.

Harvey, D. (2005) *A Brief History of Neo-Liberalism*, Oxford: Oxford University Press.

Hatje, A.-C. (1974) *Befolkningsfrågan och välfärden: Debatten om familjepolitik och nativitetsökning under 1930- och 1940-talen*, Stockholm: Allmänna förlaget.

Hatje, A.-C. (1999) *Från treklang till triangeldrama: Barnträdgården som ett kvinnligt samhällsprojekt under 1880–1940-talen*, Lund: Historiska Media.

Hermansson, J. (1993) *Politik som intressekamp: Parlamentariskt beslutsfattande och organiserade intressen i Sverige*, Stockholm: Norstedts juridik (Fritzes).

Hernes, H. (1987) *Welfare State and Woman Power: Essays in State Feminism*, Oslo: Norwegian University Press.

Hirdman, Y. (1988) 'Genussystemet – reflexioner kring kvinnors sociala underordning', *Kvinnovetenskaplig tidskrift*, vol 9, no 3, pp 49-63.

Hirdman, Y. (1989) *Att lägga livet till rätta: Studier i svensk folkhemspolitik*, Stockholm: Carlssons.

Hirdman, Y. (1990) 'Genussystemet', in SOU 1990:44 *Demokrati och makt i Sverige: Maktutredningens huvudrapport*.

Hirdman, Y. (1998) *Med kluven tunga: LO och genusordningen*, Stockholm: Atlas.

Hobson, B. (1990) 'No exit, no voice. Women's economic dependency and the welfare state', *Acta Sociologica*, vol 33, no 3, pp 235-50.

Hobson, B. (ed) (2002) *Making Men into Fathers: Men, Masculinities and the Social Politics of Fatherhood*, Cambridge: Cambridge University Press.

Jämlikhet (1969) Stockholm: SAP.

Jansson, F., Pylkkänen, E. and Valck, L. (2003) *Jämställd föräldraförsäkring? Bilaga 12 till Långtidsutredningen 2003*, Stockholm: Fritzes.

Jessop, B. (2002) *The Future of the Capitalist State*, Cambridge: Polity Press.

Johansson, J. (1991) *Det statliga kommittéväsendet: Kunskap, kontroll, konsensus*, Stockholm: Stockholm University.

Karlsson, G. (2001) *Från broderskap till systerskap: Det socialdemokratiska kvinnoförbundets kamp för inflytande och makt i SAP*, Lund: Arkiv förlag.

Kautto, M., Heikkilä, M., Hvinden, B., Marklund, S. and Ploug, N. (1999) *Nordic Social Policy, Changing Welfare States*, London: Routledge.

Kjellberg, A. (1992) 'Sweden: can the model survive?', in R. Hyman and A. Ferner (eds) *Industrial Relations in the New Europe*, Oxford: Blackwell.

Klein, V. and Myrdal, A. (1957) *Kvinnans två roller*, Stockholm: Barnängens förlag.

Klinth, R. (2002) *Att göra pappa med barn: Den svenska pappapolitiken, 1960–95*, Umeå: Boréa bokförlag.

Korpi, W. (1979) *Arbetarklassen i välfärdskapitalismen: Arbete, fackförening och politik i Sverige*, Stockholm: Prisma.

Korpi, W. (1983) *The Democratic Class Struggle*, London: Routledge & Kegan Paul.

Koven, S. and Michels, S. (eds) (1993) *Mothers of the New World: Maternalist Politics and the Origin of the Welfare State*, New York, NY: Routledge.

Landby Eduards, M. and Åström, G. (1983) '*Många kände sig manade, men få blev kallade. En granskning av arbetet för ökad kvinnorepresentation*'. Stockholm: Socialdepartementet.

Langvasbråten, T. (2008) 'A Scandinavian model? Gender equaliy discourses on mulitculturalism', *Journal of Social Politics*, vol 15, no 1, pp 32-52.

Lasch, C. (1977) *Haven in a Heartless World: The Family Besieged*, New York, NY: Basic Books.

Laskar, P. (2004) *Ett bidrag till heterosexualitetens historia: Kön, sexualitet och njutningsnormer i sexhandböcker 1800-1920*, Stockholm: Modernista.

Leira, A. (1992) *Welfare States and Working Mothers: The Scandinavian Experience*, Cambridge: Cambridge University Press.

Leira, A. (2002) *Working Parents and the Welfare State: Family Change and Policy Reform in Scandinavia*, Cambridge: Cambridge University Press.

Lewin, L. (1967) *Planhushållningsdebatten*, Stockholm: Almqvist & Wiksell.

Lewis, G. (ed) (1998) *Forming Nation, Framing Welfare*, London: Routledge/The Open University.

Lewis, J. (1992) 'Gender and the development of welfare regimes', *Journal of European Social Policy*, vol 2, no 3, pp 159-73.

Lewis, J. (ed) (1993) *Women and Social Policies in Europe*, Aldershot: Edward Elgar.

Lewis, J. (1994) 'Gender, the family and women's agency in the building of "welfare states": the British case', *Social History*, vol 19, no 1, pp 37-55.

Lewis, J. (1997) 'Gender and welfare regimes: further thoughts', *Social Politics*, vol 4, no 2, pp 160–81.

Lewis, J. (2000) 'Gender and welfare regimes', in G. Lewis, S. Gewirtz and J. Clarke (eds) *Rethinking Social Policy*, London: The Open University in association with Sage.

Lewis, J. (2001) *The End of Marriage: Individualism and Intimate Relations*, Cheltenham: Edward Elgar.

Lewis, J. (2003) *Should We Worry about Family Change?*, Toronto: University of Toronto Press.

Lewis, J. (2009) *Work–family balance, gender and policy*, Cheltenham: Edward Elgar.

Lewis, J. and Giullari, S. (2005) 'The adult worker model family, gender equality and care: the search for new policy principles and the possibilities and problems of capabilities approach', *Economy and Society*, vol 34, no 1, pp 76-104.

Liljeström, R. (1978) 'Sweden', in S.B. Kamerman and A.J. Kahn (eds) *Family Policy: Government and Families in Fourteen Countries*, New York, NY: Columbia University Press.

Liljeström, R. (1989) 'Integration of family policy and labour market policy in Sweden', in R. Steinberg Ratner (ed) *Equal Employment Policy for Women: Strategies for Implementation in the United States, Canada and Western Europe*, Philadelphia, PA: Temple University Press.

Lindqvist, R. (1989) 'Konflikt och kompromiss vid den allmänna sjukförsäkringens tillkomst', *Arkiv för studier i arbetarrörelsens historia*, no 41/42, pp 52-81.

Lister, R. (1997) *Citizenship: Feminist Perspectives*, London: Macmillan.

Lister, R. (2000) 'Gender and the analysis of social policy', in G. Lewis, S. Gewirtz and J. Clarke (eds) *Rethinking Social Policy*, London: Sage Publications.

LO (Trade Union Confederation) (1951) *Fackföreningsrörelsen och den fulla sysselsättningen* [*The Trade Union Movement and Full Employment*], Stockholm: LO.

Lundin, D., Mörck, E. and Öckert, D. (2007) *Maxtaxan inom barnomsorgen – påverkar den hur mycket föräldrar arbetar?* Rapport 2007: 2, IFAU: Uppsala.

Lundqvist, Å. (2001) *Bygden, bruket och samhället: Om människor och organisationer i brukssamhället Böksholm, 1900-1979*, Lund: Arkiv förlag.

Lundqvist, Å. (2007) *Familjen i den svenska modellen*, Umeå: Boréa bokförlag.

Lundqvist, Å. (2008) 'Family policy between science and politics', in K. Melby, A.-B. Ravn and C. Carlsson Wetterberg (eds) *Gender Equality and Welfare Politics in Scandinavia*, Bristol: The Policy Press.

Lundqvist, Å. and Roman, C. (2008) 'Construction(s) of Swedish family policy, 1930-2000', *Journal of Family History*, vol 33, no 2, pp 216-36.

Lövgren, B. (1993) *Hemarbete som politik: Diskussioner om hemarbete, Sverige 1930-40-talen, och tillkomsten av Hemmens forskningsinstitut*, Stockholm: Almqvist & Wiksell International.

Lövgren, N. (2010) *Utfall för jämställdhetsbonusen*, Stockholm: Rapport från Försäkringskassan.

Mannen i förändring. Idéprogram från arbetsgruppen om mansrollen (1985) Stockholm: Tiden/Arbetsmarknadsdepartementet.

Marklund, S. (1988) *Paradise Lost? The Nordic Welfare States and the Recession, 1975-1985*, Arkiv: Lund.

Matthiessen, L. (1970) 'Finanspolitiken som stabiliseringspolitiskt instrument', in *Svensk finanspolitik i teori och praktik*, Stockholm: Aldus, EFI och Bonniers.

Melby, K., Pylkkänen, A., Rosenbeck, B. and Carlsson Wetterberg, C. (2006) *Inte ett ord om kärlek. Äktenskap och politik i Norden ca 1850-1930*, Malmö: Makadam.

Melby, K., Ravn, A.-B. and Carlsson Wetterberg, C. (eds) (2008) *Gender Equality and Welfare Politics in Scandinavia*, Bristol: The Policy Press.

Misgeld, C., Molin, K. and Åmark, K. (1992) *Creating Social Democracy: A Century of the Social Democratic Labor Party in Sweden*, Pennsylvania: Pennsylvania State University Press.

Moberg, E. (2003[1961]) 'Kvinnans villkorliga frigivning', in E. Moberg *Prima materia: Texter i urval*, Stockholm: Ordfront.

Molyneux, M. (1979) 'Beyond the domestic labour debate', *New Left Review*, vol 116, pp 3-27.

Morgan, K.J. (2005) 'The production of child care: how labour markets shape social policy and vice versa', *Social Politics*, vol 12, no 2, pp 243-63.

Morgan, K.J. (2006) *Working Mothers and the Welfare State: Religion and the Politics Of Work-Family Policies in Western Europe and the United States*, Stanford, CA: Stanford University Press.

Mulinari, D. (2008) 'Women friendly? Understanding gendered racism in Sweden', in K. Melby, A.-B. Ravn and C. Carlsson Wetterberg (eds) *Gender Equality and Welfare Politics in Scandinavia: The Limits of Political Ambition?*, Bristol: The Policy Press, pp 167-83.

Myrdal, A. (1932) *Kollektiv bostadsform*, Tiden, December 1932.

Myrdal, A. (1944) *Folk och familj*, Stockholm: KF:s Bokförlag.

Myrdal, A. and Myrdal, G. (1934) *Kris i befolkningsfrågan*, Stockholm: Bonnier.

Nilsson, J.O. (1994) *Alva Myrdal: En virvel i den moderna strömmen*, Stockholm/Stehag: Symposion.

Nyberg, A. (2002) 'Gender, (de)commodification, economic (in)dependence and autonomous households: the case of Sweden', *Critical Social Policy. A Journal of Theory and Practice in Social Welfare*, vol 22, no 70, pp 72-96.

Nycander, S. (2002) *Makten over arbetsmarknaden: Ett perspektiv på Sveriges 1900-tal*, Stockholm: SNS förlag.

Oakley, A. (1974) *The Sociology of Housework*, London: Martin Robertson.

Ohlander, A.-S. (1992) 'The invisible child? The struggle for a social democratic family policy in Sweden, 1900-1960', in G. Bock and P. Thane (eds) *Maternity and Gender Policies: Women and the Rise of the European Welfare States 1880s-1950s*, London and New York, NY: Routledge.

Olsson, S. (1992) *Social Policy and Welfare State in Sweden*, Lund: Arkiv förlag.

Orloff, A.S. (1993) *The Politics of Pensions: A Comparative Analysis of Britain, Canada and the United States, 1880-1940*, Madison, WI: University of Wisconsin Press.

Orloff, A. (1996) 'Gender in the welfare state', *Annual Review of Sociology*, vol 22, pp 51-78.

Pateman, C. (1985) *The Problem of Political Obligation: A Critique of Liberal Theory*, Cambridge: Polity Press in association with Blackwell.

Pateman, C. (1988) *The Sexual Contract*, Stanford, CA: Stanford University Press.

Persson, G. (2008) *Min väg, mina val*, Stockholm: Albert Bonniers förlag.

Polanyi, K. (2001[1944]) *The Great Transformation. The Political and Economic Origins of our Time*, Boston, MA: Beacon Press.

Ravn, A.-B. (2008) 'Married women's right to pay taxes: debates on gender, economic citizenship and tax law reform in Denmark, 1945-83', in K. Melby, A.-B. Ravn and C. Carlsson Wetterberg (eds) *Gender Equality and Welfare Politics in Scandinavia: The Limits of Political Ambition?*, Bristol: The Policy Press, pp 63-85.

Rehnberg, B. (1999) *Till arbetsmarknadens förfogande. En personlig skildring av den svenska arbetsmarknadens utveckling*. Stockholm: Hjalmarson & Högberg.

Roman, C. (2004) *Familjen i det moderna: Sociologiska sanningar och feministisk kritik*, Malmö: Liber.

Roman, C. (2008) 'Academic discourse, social policy and the construction of new families', in K. Melby, A.-B. Ravn and C. Carlsson Wetterberg (eds) *Gender Equality and Welfare Politics in Scandinavia: The Limits of Political Ambition?*, Bristol: The Policy Press, pp 101-19.

Rothstein, B. (1986) *Den socialdemokratiska staten*, Lund: Arkiv förlag.

Rothstein, B. (1992) *Den korporativa staten: Intresseorganisationer och statsförvaltning i svensk politik*, Stockholm: Norstedts.

Rothstein, B. (1996) *The Social Democratic State: The Swedish Model and the Bureaucratic Problem of Social Reforms*, Pittsburgh, PA: University of Pittsburgh Press.

Rothstein, B. and Bergström, J. (1999) *Korporatismens fall och den svenska modellens kris*, Stockholm: SNS förlag

Runcis, M. (1998) *Steriliseringar i folkhemmet*, Stockholm: Ordfront.

Rydström, J. (2001) *Sinners and Citizens – Bestiality and Homosexuality in Sweden, 1880-1950*, Stockholm: Department of History, Stockholm University.

Sainsbury, D. (1996) *Gender, Equality and Welfare States*, Cambridge: Cambridge University Press.

Sainsbury, D. (ed) (1999) *Gender and Welfare State Regimes*, Oxford: Oxford University Press.

Sainsbury, D. (2001) 'Gender and the making of welfare states: Norway and Sweden', *Journal of Social Politics*, vol 8, no 1, pp 113-43.

Sainsbury, D. and Bergqvist, C. (2009) 'The promise and pitfalls of gender mainstreaming', *International Feminist Journal of Politics*, vol 11, no 2, pp 216-34.

Schierup, C.-U., Hansen, P. and Castles, S. (eds) (2006) *Migration, Citizenship and the European Welfare State: A European Dilemma*, Oxford: Oxford University Press.

Schmitz, E. (2007) *Systerskap som politisk handling: Kvinnors organisering i Sverige 1968 till 1982*, Lund: Department of Sociology, Lund University.

Schön, L. (2000) *En svensk ekonomisk historia*, Stockholm: SNS förlag.

Schön, L. (2010) *Vår världs ekonomiska historia. Industrialismens tidsålder*, Stockholm: SNS förlag.

Segerstedt, T. and Lundquist, A. (1949) *Människan i industrisamhället: Arbetslivet*, Stockholm: SNS förlag.

Siim, B. (2000) *Gender and Citizenship*, London: Sage Publications.

Siim, B. (2008) 'Dilemmas of citizenship – tensions between gender equality and respect for diversity in the Danish welfare state', in K. Melby, A.-B. Ravn and C. Carlsson Wetterberg (eds) *Gender Equality and Welfare Politics in Scandinavia: The Limits of Political Ambition?*, Bristol: The Policy Press, pp 149-67.

Siim, B. and Skeije, H. (2008) 'Tracks, intersections and dead ends: multicultural challenges to state feminism in Denmark and Norway', *Ethnicities* (special issue), vol 8, no 3, pp 322-44.

Silva, E.B. and Smart, C. (eds) (1999) *The New Family?*, London: Sage Publications.

Skeije, H. and Teigen, M. (2003) *Menn imellom: Mannsdominans og likestillingspolitikk.* Oslo: Gyldendal.

Skocpol, T. (1992) *Protecting Soldiers and Mothers: Political Origins of Social Policy in the United States*, Cambridge, MA: Harvard University Press.

Sommestad, L. (2001) 'Lovsång till mejerskan: om den föränderliga kvinnligheten', in U. Wikander (ed) *Det evigt kvinnliga: En historia om förändring*, Lund: Studentlitteratur.

Squires, J. (2007) *The New Politics of Gender Equality*, Basingstoke: Palgrave Macmillan.

Stanfors, M. (2007) *Mellan arbete och familj. Ett dilemma för kvinnor i 1900-talets Sverige*, Stockholm: SNS förlag.

Stevrin, P. (1978) *Den samhällsstyrda forskningen*, Stockholm: Liber förlag.

Tallberg-Broman, I. (1995) *Perspektiv på förskolans historia*, Lund: Studentlitteratur.

Therborn, G. (1989) *Borgarklass och byråkrati i Sverige*, Lund: Arkiv förlag.

Törnqvist, C. (2006) *Könspolitik på gränsen. Debatterna om varannan damernas och Thamprofessurerna*, Lund: Arkiv förlag.

Tydén, M. (2002) *Från politik till praktik. De svenska steriliseringslagarna 1935-1975*, Stockholm Studies in History 63, Stockholm: Acta Universitatis Stockholmiensis.

Walby, S. (2005) 'Gender mainstreaming: productive tensions in theory and practice', *Social Politics*, vol 12, no 3, pp 321-43.

Wærness, K. (1984) 'Caregiving as women's work in the welfare state', in H. Holter (ed) *Patriachy in a Welfare Society*, Oslo: Universitetsforlaget.

Wendt Höjer, M. (2006) *Rädslans politik. Våld och sexualitet i den svenska demokratin*, Malmö: Liber.

Verloo, M. (ed) (2007) *Multiple meanings of gender equality. A critical frame analysis of gender policies in Europe*, New York: CEU Press.

Widerberg, K. (1981) 'Gammalt patriarkat i ny förklädnad', *Kvinnovetenskaplig tidskrift*, vol 2, no 3, pp 6-26.

Widerberg, K. (1986) 'Har kvinnoforskning med jämställdhetspolitik att göra?', *Kvinnovetenskaplig tidskrift*, vol 7, no 3, pp 36-47.

Wikander, U. (1999) *Kvinnoarbete i Europa, 1789–1950: Genus, makt och arbetsdelning*, Stockholm: Atlas.

Williams, F. (1997) 'Race/ethnicity, gender and class in welfare states: a framework for comparative analysis', *Social Politics*, vol 4, no 2, pp 127-59.

Winberg, M. (2008) *Lärarinna i politikens hårda skola*, Stockholm: Albert Bonniers förlag.

Official documents

AK protocol (Andra Kammarens [Second Chamber] protokoll), 1929-69
AK motions (motioner), 1930-69
FK protocol (Första Kammarens [First Chamber] protokoll), 1929-69
FK motions (motioner), 1930-69
Motions, 1970-2009
Parliamentary protocol (Riksdagens protokoll), 1970-2009

Government Bills

Bill 1937, no. 38. *Förslag om ändring i förordningen av moderskapspenning och mödrahjälpen.*
Bill 1947, no. 220. *Förslag till lag om allmänna barnbidrag m.m.*
Bill 1960, no. 135. *Förslag om allmän familjerådgivning.*
Bill 1963, no. 62. *Förslag till ökat statligt stöd till barnstugorna.*
Bill 1978/79, no. 168. *Om föräldrautbildning och förbättringar av föräldraförsäkringen.*
Bill 1978/79, no. 175. *Förslag till lag om jämställdhet mellan kvinnor och män i arbetslivet, m.m.*
Bill 1984/85, no. 130. *Om kvinnornas villkor på arbetsmarknaden.*
Bill 1987/88, no. 105. *Mål för jämställdhetspolitiken.*
Bill 1990/91, no. 113. *Om en ny jämställdhetslag m.m.*
Bill 1993/94, no. 147. *Jämställdhetspolitiken: Delad makt – delat ansvar.*
Bill 1999/2000, no. 129. *Maxtaxa och allmän förskola m.m.*
Bill 2000/01, no. 44. *Föräldraförsäkring och föräldraledighet.*
Bill 2005/06, no. 155. *Makt att forma samhället och sitt eget liv – nya mål i jämställdhetspolitiken.*
Bill 2007/08, no. 93. *Jämställdhetsbonus – familjepolitisk reform.*
Bill 2006/07, no. 94. *Skattelättnader för hushållstjänster.*
Bill 2007/08, no. 91. *Vårdnadsbidrag. Familjepolitisk reform.*
Bill 2007/08, no. 95. *Ett starkare skydd mot diskriminering.*
Bill 2007/08, no. 149. *Vårdnadsbidrag – familjepolitisk reform.*

Reports from the Committee of Health and Welfare

2007/08:SfU10. *Jämställdhetsbonus. Familjepolitisk reform.*

Reports from the Ministry series (Ds)

Ds 2007:50. *Jämställdhetsbonus. Familjepolitisk reform.*

Memoranda

Skr. (Skrivelse) 1996/97:41. *Jämställdhetspolitiken.*
Skr. 1999/2000:2. *Jämställdhetspolitiken inför 2000-talet.*
Skr. 2002/03:140. *Jämt och ständigt Regeringens jämställdhetspolitik och handlingsplan för mandatperioden.*
Skr. 2008/09:198. *En jämställd arbetsmarknad – regeringens strategi för jämställdhet på arbetsmarknaden och i näringslivet.*

Government commission reports

SOU 1929:28. *Betänkande angående moderskapsförsäkring m.m.*
SOU 1936:12. *Betänkande angående förlossningsvården och barnmorskeväsendet samt förebyggande mödra- och barnavård. Avgivet av befolkningskommittén.*
SOU 1936:15. *Betänkande angående moderskapspenning och mödrahjälp.*
SOU 1936:59. *Betänkande i sexualfrågan. Avgivet av befolkningskommittén.*
SOU 1938:13. *Betänkande angående förvärvsarbetande kvinnors rättsliga ställning vid äktenskap och barnsbörd. Avgivet av befolkningskommittén.*
SOU 1938:20. *Betänkande angående barnkrubbor och sommarkolonier m.m.*
SOU 1938:47. *Betänkande ang. gift kvinnas förvärvsarbete m.m. avgivet av kvinnoarbetskommitténs betänkande.*
SOU 1943:9. *Utredning och förslag angående statsbidrag till daghem och lekskolor m.m.*
SOU 1944:51. *Betänkande i abortfrågan avgivet av 1941 års befolkningsutredning.*
SOU 1945:36 *Utredningar angående ekonomisk efterkrigsplanering.*
SOU 1946:5. *Betänkande om barnkostnadernas fördelning. Med förslag angående allmänna barnbidrag m.m.*
SOU 1946:23. *Socialvårdskommitténs betänkande XII: Utredning och förslag angående moderskapsbidrag.*
SOU 1947:24. *Fackföreningsrörelsen och den fulla sysselsättningen.*
SOU 1947:46. *Betänkande angående familjeliv och hemarbete. Avgivet av utredningen för hem- och familjefrågor.*
SOU 1951:15. *Daghem och förskolor. Betänkande om barnstugor och barntillsyn.*
SOU 1953:29. *Abortfrågan, Betänkande avgivet av 1950 års abortutredning.*
SOU 1954:4. *Moderskapsförsäkring m.m.*
SOU 1955:29. *Samhället och barnfamiljerna. 1954 års familjeutredning.*
SOU 1957:33. *Allmän familjerådgivning.*
SOU 1959:13. *Familjebeskattning.*
SOU 1961:38. *Stöd åt barnaföderskor.*
SOU 1964:36. *Ökat stöd till barnfamiljer.*
SOU 1967:8. *Barnstugor. Barnavårdsmannaskap. Barnolycksfall.*
SOU 1967:52. *Barnbidrag och familjetillägg.*
SOU 1972:26 och 27. *Förskolan. Del 1 och 2. Betänkandet avgivet av 1968 års barnstugeutredning.*
SOU 1972:34. *Familjestöd. Betänkandet avgivet av Familjepolitiska kommittén.*

SOU 1975:30. *Barnmiljöutredningen.*

SOU 1975:31. *Barn. Samhället och barns utveckling.*

SOU 1975:33. *Barns uppfostran och utveckling.*

SOU 1975:35. *Barnfamiljernas ekonomi.*

SOU 1975:37. *Barn och föräldrars arbete.*

SOU 1975:39. *Barnens livsmiljö.*

SOU 1975:58. *Målet är jämställdhet. En svensk rapport med anledning av FN:s kvinnoår.*

SOU 1978:5. *Föräldrautbildning. 1. Kring barnet födelse.*

SOU 1978:38. *Lag om jämställdhet i arbetslivet.*

SOU 1978: 39. *Föräldrastödsutredningen.*

SOU 1979:89. *Kvinnors arbete. Om hemarbetande kvinnors situation, kvinnor försörjning, barns omsorg och mäns delaktighet i det oavlönade hemarbetet. En rapport från jämställdhetskommittén.*

SOU 1982:18. *Förvärvsarbete och föräldraskap. Åtgärdsförslag från jämställdhetskommittén. Betänkande avgivet av Jämställdhetskommittén.*

SOU 1985:40. *Regeringen, myndigheterna och myndigheternas ledning. Huvudbetänkande från verksledningskommittén.*

SOU 1987:19. *Varannan Damernas. Slutbetänkande från utredningen om kvinnorepresentation.*

SOU 1990:41. *Tio år med jämställdhetslagen – utvärdering och förslag. Betänkande av jämställdhetsutredningen.*

SOU 1990:44. *Demokrati och makt i Sverige. Maktutredningens huvudrapport.*

SOU 1995:60. *Kvinnofrid. Del A. Huvudbetänkande av Kvinnovåldskommissionen.*

SOU 1998:6. *Ty makten är din... Myten om det rationella arbetslivet och det jämställda Sverige.*

SOU 2001:10. *Barn i homosexuella familjer.*

SOU 2005:56. *Det blågula glashuset – strukturell diskriminering i Sverige.*

SOU 2005:66. *Makt att forma samhället och sitt eget liv. Jämställdhetspolitiken mot nya mål.*

SOU 2005:73. *Reformerad föräldraförsäkring. Kärlek, omvårdnad, trygghet.*

SOU 2006:22. *En sammanhållen diskrimineringslagstiftning.*

SOU 2006:79. *Integrationens svarta bok. Agenda för jämlikhet och social sammanhållning.*

Index

Note: The letter n following a page number indicates an endnote.